MW00323903

THE
Formula

7 PRINCIPLES *to* TRANSFORM DOUBT *and* DESPAIR *into* CONFIDENCE *and* SUCCESS

DAN LEEVER

LEEVER PARTNERS

Published by:
Leever Partners
MANALAPAN, FLORIDA

Cover and interior design: Gary A. Rosenberg
www.thebookcouple.com

Printed in the United States of America

To Julie, Skip, and Alex,
who allowed me to pursue my passion
even though it sometimes resulted in my
being less available than I would like.

Contents

Introduction

recently retired as CEO of Platform Specialty Products, a large chemical company, and its predecessor company, MacDermid, after a twenty-five-year tenure. At the age of forty-two, and after many ups and downs, twists and turns, I was appointed CEO of MacDermid. From that time, the company grew its revenue from $150 million to $4 billion. Its value increased more than fiftyfold. Truly, it was one of the great value-creation stories in our industry.

MacDermid was a specialty chemical company that made chemical formulations in small quantities for small niche applications. We made the chemicals auto manufacturers used to plate chrome on car bumpers and electronic manufacturers used to produce circuit boards.

All that said, I have spent as much of my life feeling like a big failure as I did experiencing growth and success. I was able to turn the insecurities and mistakes of my early life and career into something fulfilling and fantastic, and it is still a daily practice to maintain the new state of mind and clarity I have today. Looking back, I found a formula, something I could experiment with, alter, expand upon, and finally commit to after much trial and error. That formula, the one that changed my life and continues to keep me motivated and productive, is the subject of this book. It is my opinion that, if followed, this formula can help make anyone's wildest dreams come true and, at the very least, give them a path to a wholesome journey that will leave them fulfilled.

Such a formula, based on solid science, exists. I know because it has transformed me into who I am today. Many other people from different walks of life have used it, too. All have benefitted from its power. In the pages to follow, in addition to my story, you will learn about some of my heroes, some famous and some not, who illustrate the principles of The Formula that took me from shy, unconfident, and learning disabled to a world-class business leader. If you apply these principles as instructed, you, too, will achieve results beyond your wildest dreams. The power of The Formula is not limited to the world of business. It can be applied just as successfully to sports, nonprofit activities, or personal pursuits—anything you aspire to and deem worthwhile. This is because these are life principles, not just business principles. Not only can these principles take you to a higher level personally, they can also be applied to any organization to which you belong. My hope is that by sharing these lessons and principles, you will find the pathway to happiness and success that took me a lifetime to learn.

The skills and attitudes found in The Formula work no matter when you start to use them or how deep a hole from which you struggle. My personal story shared in the following pages will prove to you that you can be in an incredibly challenging mental state, one of darkness, but through living certain principles, the light will emerge and guide you to turn your life around.

You can eliminate the lack of confidence that prevents you from trying risky activities to start with. Anxiety? The Formula can help you mitigate it. Yes, there is a step-by-step formula to reach the stars. Maybe you have been languishing, not knowing success or defeat, just existing. The Formula will give you a road map to fill the void forever.

I discovered The Formula out of necessity, of having to climb out of the depths of constant challenge, self-doubt, and shame. Life wasn't always so easy for me. But, if I was able to be successful in spite of my limitations, you can do the same.

PART ONE

The Principles of The Formula

CHAPTER 1

PRINCIPLE 1:
Have the Guts to Fail

*Far better is it to dare mighty things, to win glorious
triumphs, even though checkered by failure . . .
than to rank with those poor spirits who neither
enjoy nor suffer much, because they live in a gray
twilight that knows not victory nor defeat.*

—THEODORE ROOSEVELT

I was a poster child for failure. My first real experience with failure happened when I was held back in third grade. Poor grades were again to blame the second time I was held back, before I made it out of grammar school. I concluded I was stupid—a notion from which no one in my early life had ever tried to disabuse me. I remember sitting for hours with my mother, reviewing flashcards with simple spelling words and math tables to help me learn them. I remember closing my eyes and trying as hard as I could to commit them to memory. But, as hard as I tried, I would spend hours, days on end, and nothing, literally nothing, would stick. The next day in school, I'd still come away with Ds or Fs. My brain just didn't work the way other people's did.

Eventually my parents took me to a psychologist who conducted a battery of tests and recommended I be sent to a vocational school where I could learn to do something with my hands, rather than my mind. In sixth grade, I was sent to Rumsey Hall, a boarding school specializing in intimate class settings and individual support. It was a positive experience, but it didn't fix whatever it was that was "wrong" with me.

Today, more than sixty years later, I understand that I had several undiagnosed learning disabilities. Schools today know how to diagnose and treat these disabilities, but in the 1950s, when I was a little kid, they did not. If your grades stank, you were presumed to be dumb or lazy—and since I wasn't lazy, that left dumb. It turns out that my learning disabilities were partly due to a severe imbalance between the two hemispheres of my brain.

We know that there are two types of processing. The first is explicit processing, often referred to as left-brain thinking, which is rule-based, sequential, conscious processing. This kind of thinking is the capability that helps make a person successful in school. The second is implicit processing, which is evidenced by intuition, unconscious thought, automaticity, creativity, and lateral thinking. So, in other words, I was born with a natural mental orientation that emphasized implicit processing, sometimes referred to as right-brain thinking. While most people have the ability to utilize both sides of the brain to perform a specific, relative process, my right brain was so dominant that it was as if my left brain was asleep.

With regard to my mental processing, assuming the average person uses the explicit left brain and implicit right brain almost equally (50/50), I have come to believe that I was about 90 percent right brain and 10 percent left brain.

My implicit right brain works fine—better than fine. Literally and figuratively, I've always been able to see the big picture and see it quicker and more clearly than most people. I have the ability to process lots of information all at once. I can look at a complex situation and make sense of it in an instant. Understanding how the trees fit into the forest has always been my strength. For example, in my field of expertise, business strategy and finance, I can spot trends in financial statements often long before others. I might not be able to calculate the math, but I can make sense of it. As for my ability to concentrate on one tree to the next? Not so much. Even today I struggle to do such things as simple math, keep track of appointments, or write messages without leaning heavily on spell check.

As a child, no one in my support system, including my parents and teachers, recognized or understood these characteristics. So, I just struggled on, failing over and over, becoming more frustrated and less confident. I did excel in one thing, though—sports. Not only did I have the physical credentials to be an athlete—physique, speed, endurance—I also found I could easily marshal the huge amounts of drive and passion needed to achieve more than I ever thought possible. As a football running back, I could routinely carry multiple defensemen before being brought down. I was ultimately tackled, not because I gave up, but because it was impossible to move forward with so many tacklers hanging on my back.

Through a commitment to weight training, I developed great strength, which allowed me to play any position on the football field and, in fact, often did. Playing sports and doing well athletically gave me confidence and also taught me that I could be a leader. I discovered I could inspire teammates, literally infecting them with my belief in my reality until they adopted that reality as their own, even if the facts were stacked against us. Yes, we could defeat the undefeated team! I so believed in my vision of what was possible that my teammates came to believe it, too.

I have since learned that only a few, rare business leaders have had this same capability, including, most famously, Steve Jobs. Jobs was said to be able to project a "reality distortion field," meaning that when people were in his presence, they found themselves under a kind of spell that caused them to see the world the way Jobs did, whether or not that vision comported with their own preexisting understanding of reality. Whether you are trying to lead people on the playing field, on the shop floor, or in battle, this trait, which can be learned, is valuable. Now back to my story.

I was striking out in academics, but at the same time, I was scoring points in sports. In sixth grade, I tried out for the hockey team. The only problem was I couldn't skate. The players laughed at me. Ultimately, I didn't make the team. But that winter I learned to skate. Boy, did I skate! I skated nonstop every chance I got. I even used to sneak out of my dorm after midnight and skate in the dark for hours on the rink. Believe me, the next winter no one laughed at me. Eventually, I was the captain of the varsity hockey team. I am a huge believer in nurture over nature. I believe my limitations in academics provided a narrower outlet for me to experience success, so by necessity, I worked much harder than my peers at sports. That success provided incentive for me to work even harder, and I got even better. A virtuous cycle ensued.

In football, the coach used to play me only part of the game, because against languid prep-school boys, my intensity was almost unfair; I just scared the hell out of them. On defense I played middle linebacker, but I lived in the other team's backfield, because everyone was afraid to block me.

My success in sports, I have come to understand, was due

mostly to my passion and ability to get others to believe, as well as my ethic for hard work and capacity for leadership and commitment. I would never have predicted that what I was learning on the sports field would be critical to who I became later. Sports—and all their glorious and gut-wrenching facets—were my learning ground for life.

I was co-MVP of the football team at Watertown High School, in Connecticut, where I grew up. Years later, when my coach, Bill Gargano, spoke at the ceremony at which I was inducted into the Watertown High School Football Hall of Fame, he reminisced by saying he wasn't sure he'd ever coached anybody more intense than me in his thirty-five years of coaching. "When our Creator was handing out the energy pills," Coach said, "he must have skipped somebody and given Dan two."

In high school and college, I bumped along, succeeding in sports and struggling in academics. The belief that my academic difficulties were an indication of my not being smart stood firmly with me. And then my failure to finish college only confirmed the negative picture I had painted of myself. Although I attended college for four years, I couldn't find a way to pass the more left-brain-oriented classes, like math and statistics, and ultimately gave up and left without a degree.

Going to college was partly an effort to please my father, but there, too, I felt I came up short. Like me, Dad had been an outstanding athlete, captain of his high school football team and star quarterback. But, unlike me, he hadn't stopped there. He had been a National Merit Scholar and graduated from Michigan State as a chemical engineer, all while supporting himself during the Depression! In 1950 he became CEO of MacDermid, which at the time was a small chemical company, where he enjoyed a deep following among his colleagues.

Down the Drain

I had always been interested in business. My father had a practice of inviting traveling businessmen to our house for dinner. There were many business talks over the dinner table in my formative years, which, I believe, ignited my interest. I suppose business was in my blood. I took business classes in college and attended the summer sales meetings of MacDermid, further piquing my interest. Around the same time I dropped out of college, I decided to pursue a career in business. At first I tried a job as an industrial salesman traveling a four-state area in the Midwest. It was fun to travel on an expense account, and I learned a lot by visiting many companies in my territory, even though I was no great shakes at sales. After a couple years, I quit and opened a small retail shop that sold consumer telecommunications gear such as phones and answering machines. My brother, Andy, who had just finished high school, joined me, and together we enjoyed decent volume. I quickly realized that no matter how much we sold out of this one shop, we were never going to make very much money. One small store just couldn't do enough volume; we couldn't scale. About all we could expect was to pay ourselves a small salary. Scale matters.

We received requests from customers to repair telecommunications gear, so with Andy's being handy, we grew our business to become almost 100 percent profit service work. I learned margins matter.

We bought our inventory from various manufacturers, distributors, and importers, but noticed that most of what we were selling was made in Asia. So, we tracked down companies in Asia that could supply us. I took trips to Japan, Korea, and Taiwan, and, by attending trade shows and talking to trading companies, I found several factories my brother and

I could buy from. The only problem was that the minimum quantities were too high for our single retail store. That's when we decided to start a wholesale business, competing with the importers from whom we had been buying to supply our retail store.

This was a bootstrap operation if there ever was one. I would go to Asia and buy the equipment while my brother watched the store and continued with repairs. We worked with a local advertising agency to design marketing materials and packaging. I hit the road during the week to solicit and sell to new and existing retailers, and on the weekends, I would package and ship orders, and then do it all over again the next week. We called the company Leever Brothers, a takeoff on the consumer products company Lever Brothers, and therefore appeared much bigger than we were. Perception matters. Our customers included Sears, Macy's, and other large retailers.

You're probably wondering how someone who was not very good in sales suddenly began selling to huge companies like Sears. I believe the difference is passion. When I was selling industrial lubricants and chemicals, fresh out of college, it was too far outside my comfort zone to exhibit passion. After having sold telecommunications products out of my retail store for a couple years, I learned in a small-scale, controlled environment. If I screwed up the pitch, I lost the sale of one phone, no big deal. After two years of learning to sell, one phone at a time, I was ready to express myself in a persuasive environment. I became passionate about my newly developed ability to sell my ideas. I realized that this skill could be used much more broadly than selling a single phone. Buyers felt my passion and gave our little company the benefit of the doubt.

One thing led to another, and the business ended up a small-scale national success. I was having a blast. More important, I began to see that I could be good at something—that it was possible for me not to be a failure.

For the first time in my life, now in my late twenties, I developed a degree of self-confidence. True, I still had deficits, and I knew I was different from other people, but I started to understand that part of that difference meant that I possessed gifts others didn't. In the office, I found a way to cope with my mental limitations: it was called having an assistant. So what if I had trouble remembering appointments or writing letters? My assistant could do those things for me. I learned that I could compensate for my deficiencies by recruiting people who had the talents I lacked.

It was during this period I discovered that some of the same attributes that had worked for me on the football field could also work in business. I again harnessed my passion to create a reality distortion field. I learned that customers could feel my passion—and they really liked it! I could sell a concept to my coworkers with such fervor that I would win a level of commitment and loyalty from them that exceeded my expectations.

Part of my coworkers' loyalty, I think, came straight from my being so vulnerable. It's pretty hard for people to question your sincerity or doubt your motives when you are honest about your weaknesses and when they see you struggling so hard to overcome them. For instance, I never thought of my coworkers as employees. We were all colleagues. The fact that my brother and I owned the company was irrelevant in our minds. We were all rowing the boat. I carried this philosophy for the rest of my career. And, yes, I was an owner, but I still struggled with day-to-day activities. Being honest with my coworkers about my struggles won me their empathy and trust. Then I could inspire the team to create win-wins for all of us.

All of this was great fun and a great run. For the first time in my life, I felt I had put my stupid self behind me and placed my failures in context. I started to believe that, yes, I was different, but maybe not different in a bad way. Maybe I wasn't stupid; maybe I just functioned differently. I began to see that the passion and strategic perspective, or "forest for the trees," might be a gift. Over time I began to believe I could develop my traits. It wouldn't be until sometime later that this insight became ingrained, but hope was starting to emerge.

Then, after six good years, the phone industry changed. Our unique service was no longer unique. As the major telecommunications manufacturers entered the market, Leever Brothers was overwhelmed by their power and huge financial assets. I didn't see any of this coming. There was no way we could compete with the huge manufacturers. Our business cratered. Everything I'd worked so hard for went down the drain. Although I didn't file for bankruptcy, I might just as well have. Six years of effort, twelve hours a day, seven days a week, and I had nothing to show for it. At the age of thirty, I woke up feeling that all I had to show for my life were some dusty sports trophies.

My hard-won, new self-confidence vanished instantly. All I could think was, *If only I'd done this, if only I'd done that . . . if only, if only.* I concluded, *I was lucky for a while. But in the end the real me showed through.*

Introspection and depression paralyzed me. I was so low in self-esteem, so depressed, and so little a believer in myself that I couldn't function. I didn't get out of bed. I stopped doing simple but necessary things, like paying bills, grocery shopping, and answering the phone. This went on for about a year. During this period my wife left me, having given up on me. While I was separated, I didn't have a place to live so

I broke into a shed that belonged to friends who were away for the summer. I slept there for months until my wife and son moved out of our apartment, and I moved back in.

Physical survival became my sole imperative. *Gotta eat,* I'd say to myself. *Can't eat if you don't get out of bed.* I could have reached out to my parents, but I was too ashamed. In my slough of despair I asked myself, *Where can I get a job where I can be stupid? Where can I still do everything wrong and not have anyone notice?* In a flash the answer came to me: Sambo's, a restaurant that was located right down the street from the apartment.

Recipe for Lifesaving:
Pickles, Onions, Lettuce, Cheese

I got hired into what Sambo's called its management-training program. Through the process, I discovered I was not completely worthless. *Hey! I can cut up lettuce as good as the next guy—maybe better. So, it's not like I can't do anything . . .* Plus, sometimes the smaller the thing you focus on, the easier it is to succeed. It's hard to find something less significant than chopping lettuce.

I moved from lettuce to waiting tables. Customers liked me. My self-confidence grew each time I connected with a new customer. One thing led to another. I had these tiny successes. And, after a while, I started to feel I was getting back at least a little control over my life.

Maybe there's hope for me, I started to think. *I have to learn to work with what I've got, not obsess over what I don't. Maybe I have limitations in some areas, and maybe, just maybe, these weaknesses are at least partly counterbalanced by strengths. I'm just different.* I also began to realize that my mental health was a delicate thing, and it was going to be my responsibility to guard it and take charge of it. I accepted my situation. I began to own it.

I didn't know it at the time, but Steve Jobs had also struggled with failures, many larger ones than mine, before he was able to build Apple into what it is today.

Jobs himself had this to say, in part, in his 2005 commencement address at Stanford University:

> *I'm pretty sure none of this would have happened if I hadn't been fired from Apple. It was awful tasting medicine, but I guess the patient needed it. Sometimes life hits you in the head with a brick. Don't lose faith. I'm convinced that the only thing that kept me going was that I loved what I did. You've got to find what you love.*[1]

I might not necessarily have stumbled on what I loved, but at Sambo's, I continued to enjoy modest successes. I progressed from assistant manager to manager. I used my reality distortion field so that pretty soon I had a devoted team working with me. Our store went from being one of the lowest in revenue in the chain to one of the highest. I was really beginning to feel like I was figuring life out.

---

1   Jobs, Steve. "Commencement Address at Stanford University (2005)." Genius. Accessed August 20, 2018. genius.com/Steve-jobs-commencement-address-at-stanford-university-2005-annotated.

CHAPTER 2

PRINCIPLE 2:
Embrace Your Uniqueness

*No one can make you feel inferior
without your consent.*

—Eleanor Roosevelt

The Sambo's chain tanked in 1982, but somehow I felt ready for a change. After that, I followed in my father's footsteps and joined MacDermid where I was to spend the next thirty-plus years. In 1982 MacDermid was a small but successful specialty chemical company heavily dominated by business in the United States. Founded in 1922 by Archie MacDermid, a Scottish immigrant, the company was already sixty years old. My father had been CEO from 1950 to 1980 and was still chairman of the board, although not active in the day-to-day business.

The CEO in those days was an MBA graduate of an Ivy League business school. He hired me—to my father's chagrin, as my father really did not believe in nepotism, especially given my checkered background. Being hired at that point was not a big risk for the CEO, as I made less than his secretary. He hired me as a low-paid analyst on a three-month trial basis. I initially did gofer-type work, nothing substantive. Honestly, it wasn't much of a leap from Sambo's.

I performed simple analyses of projects the CEO was considering for investment. One of the first was a proposal to build mini plants around the country to recycle waste from our customers' processes. There was a strong push from the management team to make this investment. My analysis did not support that view. Surprisingly, my analysis proved right and saved the company a lot of money. It was my first big proof at MacDermid that, even without any real experience in the mechanics of the business, I could "think outside the box," see the big picture without getting caught up in the details. But that wasn't all. I did far more work analyzing the data, dug deeper, and wouldn't take no for an answer when asking for information to help the analysis. I worked on lots of projects more or less as the CEO's staff analyst. I learned a great deal in a hurry.

One thing I never had a problem with was laziness. At MacDermid I immediately differentiated myself by taking on anything that needed doing. It was hard work, but still far less than the workload at Leever Brothers. Owners think differently than employees do. I never thought of myself as an employee and thought deeply, like an owner, about everything. At first I felt pretty inferior to all the smart folks at MacDermid. But, over time, I realized by working harder than anyone else, I could overcome whatever perceived deficit I had.

I became involved in MacDermid's fledgling international operations, first in South Africa, then in Asia, and eventually I ran all our overseas operations. I was scared to death that my critical flaw, whatever it was, would creep out and take me down again. Yes, I was feeling better and better, but I was still scared. Searching for help, I attended a "power of positive thinking" seminar and sporadically read works by success authors such as Dr. Norman Vincent Peale, Denis Waitley, and Zig Ziglar. Before long the most powerful concept of all became clear to me: cultivation of my mental health and avoidance of the demons of self-doubt were within my control. This may have been the most important realization of my entire life: "If it's to be, it's up to me!"

As the fact of control and accountability became apparent, I became obsessed with success principles. Eventually I was introduced to Brian Tracy, a very prolific success practitioner. I read his materials, listened to his tapes, and watched his videos. Over the next five years, I read anything I could get my hands on. I became completely immersed in the material until I became something of a lay expert on the subject of self-motivation and actualization. I have been a student of these principles ever since—some thirty-plus years.

Tracy indoctrinated me to success principles, many of which formed the nucleus of The Formula. I learned from him, "If it's to be, it's up to me." There is no such thing as destiny. *We* are in control and have free will to make choices that will determine our future. Tracy reinforced the concept of programming our mind, especially using positive affirmations in goal setting. I started feeding my brain. I read (slowly) countless books on ancient philosophy. I studied business, reading inspirational books like *Sam Walton: Made in America* by Sam Walton and John Huey, and the writings of Warren Buffett. Over time, my mind became adept at understanding and implementing winning business principles, many of which I cover in the chapters to follow.

Upswing

In 1982 MacDermid was facing challenges. Our end markets were becoming more competitive, and we were competing against huge companies. By 1990, the company had stagnated. Earnings per share weren't just flat; they hadn't moved in more than five years. We barely covered our cost of capital, and, as a result, even during one of the most raging bull markets in history, the stock market had not rewarded us. The stock market, as Warren Buffett has often pointed out, is sometimes anything but clear-sighted and efficient. In this instance, however, it understood our weaknesses only too well.

But, in contrast to Leever Brothers, MacDermid had the critical mass to compete with the behemoths. The Formula principles, although informal at this point, were starting to crystallize. I began mental programming by setting goals and writing affirmations in the morning. I understood we could compete with the industry giants, but not by doing the same things the same way. We were small, but we began to use our size as our advantage—our differentiator. A small company can move quickly. Our international business was *really* small. We were under the radar of even our own company, never mind our large competitors.

Because of our small size, we moved with lightning speed in our international operations. We could decide which projects to back for which customer without meetings, red tape, or tedious channels. Our managers were empowered to make decisions on the spot. The faster we moved, the more success we had, and we accelerated that with a good dousing of passion. For me, MacDermid became a calling, not a job.

Being small can be a real advantage. Large companies, by their very nature, are less risky. That is because they typically have many product lines to spread the risk. If any one product line fails, others will still exist. In a small company, often-times, business is concentrated in one or two product lines. If one of them fails, the entire company could be in trouble. The offset to that is that large companies move slowly. In theory, small companies can change and adapt to changes in the market much faster than large ones can. The problem at MacDermid was that our domestic operations, which made up the bulk of the company in those days, acted too much like a large company.

Around the same time, I felt I needed more tools in my toolbox. There was a business school at a local university that specialized in providing opportunities to older students who were employed. With a strong endorsement by our CEO, I was accepted to attend business school at night at the University of New Haven in Connecticut. Whereas the class makeup of students was nontraditional, made up of mid-career types, I was even more so—a non-college graduate with learning disabilities. I was so hungry for knowledge, I would demand from the professors that they keep the materials relevant. It made me crazy when they slipped in academic jargon and esoteric subjects we would never use. However, I could tell it bugged the traditionalists in my class. And, honestly, they were at least partly right. With all my success, I have often found that I was too impatient. A professor going off track for a while didn't seem like the end of the world. All my adult life my passion has been a double-edged sword, the source of my success and a point of stress in all my relationships.

After the first semester, my MBA classmates went to the dean, Dr. M. L. McLaughlin, and basically said, "We've got this guy in our class who's just too weird for us—too outspoken, too wound up, too brash, unstable, and controversial." They meant me. "Can't you please get rid of him?"

She told the group they would have to talk with me about it, so they did. During a holiday party the group lambasted me, saying, "You're just too weird. We don't like you. We don't like your attitude." I was devastated. I dropped out.

Six months later, another MBA class started. Dr. M. L. McLaughlin helped me connect with that class. Amazingly, this new class was full of weirdos—nontraditionalists—just like me! The second class became known by the professors as a class that would engage with them at an unusual level. Instead of sitting back in class and taking the material in, we actively engaged with the professors and debated issues. As a result, as the word spread, the best professors, who were also the most self-confident, volunteered to teach our class. No one was afraid to challenge each other or the professors. We all brought our experiences to the classroom to bring alive the academic materials. We pushed past traditional thinking to think deeply about concepts. We presented our views passionately. It resulted in a higher level of process and understanding and much more relevant education. The result was a synergy that created a spontaneous learning environment. We had a blast for the next year and a half.

Dr. M. L. McLaughlin and I developed a deep friendship. We would have lunch regularly and discuss our lives. She really encouraged me to embrace my uniqueness, which gave me strength. After all, if the dean of a business school thought I was okay, my uniqueness couldn't be all bad. I would go to her with business issues I was struggling with, and she would offer advice. At the same time she used me as a sounding board. It was a real learning experience for me to hear M. L. talk through her issues. At the same time I was honored she would even consider my opinion. She was great in advising me, and I consider her my second mentor, to whom I will forever be grateful.

Meanwhile, back at MacDermid, the more I got to know the domestic side of business, the less I liked it. Our overseas operations were entrepreneurial, lean, and profitable; however, the stateside business was top heavy with managers and choked by bureaucracy. Instead of focusing on customers, the stateside operation had an internally focused culture with layers of management attending to itself. There were committees that had committees. Our policy manual was many inches thick.

It was as if the international business was an entirely different company. Our international managers felt empowered and took risks by trying new approaches and tactics. I will never forget the time I visited our Spanish company and was informed by the management team that there was an "Iberian peninsula" recession going on (a recession limited to Spain and Portugal). They then outlined the strategies they had *already* implemented. We had successfully modified our strategy before I was even aware there was a recession going on. If this had happened in our domestic business, months of meetings would have taken place to decide whether there was a recession.

Then and now, my tendency has always been to think like an owner—to take waste and inefficiency personally and to get angry about it. To me, waste is a form of stealing from the shareholders. This single principle can be a huge differentiator. It is extremely rare for companies, especially large ones, to inculcate this cultural principle. Everyone treating the company's money as if it were their own is a powerful thing. (Think of travel. How often do folks travel on vacation the same way they do on business? Rarely, I assure you.)

Facing reality is really important. Denying reality is a sure path to mediocrity. Around 1990, with the domestic side of MacDermid in disarray, it also was characterized by an unwillingness to face the reality of what was really happening within our markets and to our customers. The domestic operations, which made up the bulk of the company, were floundering. The lack of performance in the domestic business was magnified by the economy, which in 1990, was in a recession. Tom Smith, our largest investor, told the CEO he was selling his stock because he had lost confidence in management. Upon his initial approach to them, he was told the lackluster sales were due to the economy, but it was not Tom's style to accept excuses and lack of accountability.

A small company like MacDermid had options, and Tom called us out on not using our creativity and strength to discover what those options were and capitalize on them. But my father, who was still nonexecutive chairman of the board, knew losing Tom as a shareholder would be a huge loss in prestige, so he couldn't accept Tom's position. So my father put the blame for underperformance squarely on Tom's shoulders, telling Tom, "You have not asked tough-enough questions that would have caused us to change. You have an obligation now to join our board and help us get it right."

In essence, my father's largest shareholder threatens to sell his shares because he lost confidence in the company, and my father somehow made him accept his own accountability. To this day, I have never heard of someone turning so bad of a situation into a good one. And boy, did it turn out good.

Never the man to back down from a challenge nor shirk accountability, Tom Smith joined the board. The international operations were already a highly visible success. Because I worked overseas, stateside management didn't know me well. While I was vice president of international, I was invited to a meeting of the administrative management group, whose members were responsible for the policy manual. I blurted out that I disapproved of the way each one of them ran the domestic business, and if I ever became CEO, I would run things differently. I told them they better hope I never got that job because I would be their worst nightmare.

Shortly after Tom joined the board, our CEO announced his retirement and laid out a plan: I would become chief operating officer (COO) and another executive would become chief administrative officer (CAO). After a transition period, the CEO decided to retire even earlier, so either COO (me) or the CAO would be appointed in his place. The CAO represented the status quo. I was the rebel. If this had been normal times, the CEO would have gone with the status quo. I was just too controversial. But, in the middle of a recession with an influential board member pushing for performance, more of the same was not the answer. Clearly, I received a battlefield promotion. Due to the underperformance of the company, which was now accelerated by the economy, business as usual was *not* called for.

I got the job, and I kept my promise to the domestic side and became their worst nightmare. How could I be their worst nightmare when I place such emphasis on team? Well, given the right attitude, people can become great if provided the right environment. As soon as I was promoted to CEO, I went to this group of people and laid out what needed to change, mostly focusing on eliminating waste and promoting entrepreneurialism. I talked to each person individually and let each know there was serious change afoot. MacDermid wouldn't survive if we didn't dramatically improve profitability.

When I met with the managers individually, alas, virtually none of them was willing to change. They just banded together and fought the change. Building the culture of performance in a company necessitates everyone rowing in the same direction. The result? The administrative management group was eliminated, and virtually every member of the group was fired or quit within a year of my promotion.

Deviants Become MacDermid's Norm

I am a huge believer in hiring and promoting for attitude. We hired and promoted a lot of young people. Our CFO was thirty years old when he first got promoted. Later, another of our CFOs (there were several throughout my twenty-five years at the helm) was an internal promotion from a lower-level accounting manager who rose rapidly through a series of promotions. Our president never graduated from college. One of the best was a young man who joined us out of business school and, within a year, was a corporate officer. One of my closest associates started at MacDermid right out of high school and ended up running our compensation systems and managing our capital expenditures. She ran circles around the various highly educated "professional" HR managers (I have never met an effective professional HR manager), and we inherited finance managers from acquired companies.

Our general counsel was a chemical engineer, research associate, who went to school at night to become a lawyer. Today, he is a state judge in Connecticut. One young associate ran our $100 million pension while in his twenties. We attended a seminar in which the speaker asked rhetorically, "Why don't people post job openings like, Wanted: A Really Cool . . ." I thought that was an interesting idea so my associate and I ran an advertisement in the *Wall Street Journal.* "Wanted: Really Cool Financial Executive." From that ad we hired a young man who ended up president of the company.

I could write a whole chapter about these heroes, who at other companies often would have been misfits. It started with me, as unlikely a CEO candidate as you will find.

Discovering our uniqueness was part of our new culture. One of my favorite stories is the time we were trying to acquire a competitor that was owned by a large Mexican company. I wasn't able to get through by phone to the CEO of the Mexican company, so I sent him a message that I was coming to

Mexico City, invitation or not. I arrived at his office in Mexico City and waited until he would see me. He proceeded to show me a competitive offer from our archenemy. He also emphasized he would not accept an offer with any conditions. It had to be a straight cash only, not a conditional offer. I realized we could not meet the competitive offer. After momentarily pondering what to do, I submitted a much higher offer, but it included a long list of conditions. I was betting he would fold my letter in half and show our competitor just the price, not the conditions to get them to raise the offer. That's exactly what happened. The price was so high that after our competitor bought them, the competitor was saddled with too much debt and never prospered again.

With this group of unusual characters, we performed far beyond our expectations, and for sure had one of—if not the best—long-term track records in our industry.

CHAPTER 3

PRINCIPLE 3:
Dream Big

So many of our dreams at first seem impossible,
then they seem improbable, and then, when we
summon the will, they soon become inevitable.

—Christopher Reeve

Passion is a cornerstone of performance. But without dreams it is impossible to unleash passion. The bigger the dream, the more passion is possible. It sounds difficult, but it turns out when it comes to dreaming really big, we are hardwired to do so.

Biologically, we are preprogrammed to be goal-seeking organisms. There are powerful neural chemicals that can only be accessed when you are outside your comfort zone. Effectively, your comfort zone works like a magnet. Think of the magnet as a circle with a positive charge. You are a negative charge, like a magnet and a piece of metal. When you are within the circle, the positive and negative charge is in balance and there is no stress. But what happens when you move the negative charge away from the positive charged magnet? There is tension trying to get the positive and negative charge back together. That is what happens physiologically to you when you first try new and challenging things. You experience an elevated heart rate, sweaty palms, and nervousness. You feel uncomfortable. However, your comfort zone is not static.

Imagine a simple task like catching a ball. What if you are asked to catch a ball in public, but you hadn't ever done that before? That would be way outside your comfort zone. You would get nervous and have to concentrate to achieve the task. Then imagine that you practiced tossing the ball a thousand times a day for a year. If you were then asked to do the same task of catching a ball in public, it would be far less stressful. What's happening here? You just expanded your comfort zone.

The feeling of nervousness when you are outside your comfort zone is caused by neurochemicals in your brain. The comfort zone, sometimes called homeostasis, in some cases can be good. After all, normalcy in some respects, like regulating body temperature, is essential for our survival. For instance, we wouldn't want breathing to be stressful. However, when we are in the comfort zone, by nature, nothing changes. It means when our muscles reach homeostasis, we don't run faster, jump higher, lift more, or improve in physical activities. This is true even though we have far more inherent potential than we are currently using. Mentally, when we are in the comfort zone, we don't grow. We don't get smarter or process information better or communicate better. We feel stuck in a rut, which Earl Nightingale, the famous broadcaster and motivational speaker, called "a grave with the ends kicked out."[2] Yes, we feel comfortable, but we are depriving ourselves of a large part of our humanness—the adaption and evolution to ever higher capabilities and achievements.

---

2 Nightingale, Earl. "Acres of Diamonds." Nightingale-Conant. Accessed August 20, 2018. www.nightingale.com/articles/acres-of-diamonds/.

Dreaming big takes us out of our comfort zone and activates powerful brain chemicals, especially when pursuing goals that greatly aid us in moving forward in a positive direction toward the big dream. There is a significant difference between a dream and a goal. You might think of a dream as a vision—"I want to be a concert violinist"—when you are an amateur in the beginning stages. The step is just too far by itself. Your subconscious will just say, *Nah, you're no concert violinist.* But if your goal is to practice deliberately for two hours a day, your subconscious can embrace that. The dream by itself won't trigger the neurochemicals needed to activate the dream. The goals break down the dream in manageable bites that will activate them. Don't get me wrong—you need the dream to conceptualize the goals. The dream is the "why." It activates overarching passion. Goals act as the compass that guides our progress.

Why dream big? Because it is our nature to take baby steps. With big dreams, we have the chance to break through incrementalism. Let's be clear here: incremental steps are really good when they are pointed toward an overarching goal, but it is the dream that is always driving us.

The nineteenth-century philosopher Henry David Thoreau said, "If one advances confidently in the direction of his dreams, and endeavors to live the life which he has imagined, he will meet with a success unexpected in common hours." Which means that remaining in the perceived safety of the comfort zone is inherently limiting.

In a famous experiment that tested the limits of the comfort zone, fleas were put into a bottle with a top on it. The fleas jumped—as fleas do—hitting against the lid. In no time at all, they learned to jump just high enough to avoid hitting the lid. When the top to the container was removed, the fleas, which all had the ability to jump ten times higher, kept jumping to the preestablished height. They had trained themselves to contain their natural abilities.

This conditioning is true for the human being. Unless you challenge yourself (and absent some new stimulus or incentive), you will stay within your comfort zone and your dreams will never be achieved. You will actually condition yourself to be limited. You will live inside a bottle with a top on it!

How to Escape the Comfort Zone Trap

Escaping from your comfort zone starts with belief and willingness to challenge the status quo. Take the four-minute mile. For hundreds of years, running a mile in four minutes was believed to be impossible, and scientists had plenty of facts with which to support that belief. The human body lacked the necessary lung capacity, our bone structure was all wrong, etc.

Everyone except British runner Roger Bannister believed the experts. Bannister believed in himself. And, one day in 1954, Roger Bannister ran a sub four-minute mile. The year after Bannister did it, thirty-seven other runners did it, too. And the year after that, 300 runners. What does this tell us?

We become what we expect.

So, dreaming ever bigger dreams and setting ever more ambitious goals are the prerequisites to breaking free from the prison of the comfort zone. But—and this is a *big* but— your dreams can be lofty and your goals out of this world, but at the same time you need to build them step by step to realism. We do that by having subgoals we can activate. To say you want to be on Broadway when you have never put on a pair of dancing shoes would be more of a wish than a dream or a big goal.

I have heard the argument that it is irresponsible to encourage folks to pursue low-probability goals because they might waste large amounts of time and effort on something they never achieve and might be disappointed that they fell short. But there is a powerful counterargument. Chasing our dreams has little to do with *achieving* our dreams. It is all about the journey. It's the process of striving that makes us excited to get out of bed every day when in the pursuit. Honestly, it can turn out better when we strive and fall short because the pursuit of the prize can make us more fulfilled than the achievement of the result. Some world-class performers use cascading goals to stay on the striving track; they achieve a mini goal and immediately begin the pursuit of an even higher one.

What if you aren't sure what your goal is yet? Passion is an underlying factor that helps us in determining our goals, which is why passion—finding it, using it, preserving it, and nurturing its further growth—is one of the ingredients of The Formula and will be covered more thoroughly in the next chapter.

What if you are struggling with devising a large goal? Ask yourself: "Is there something that's my dominant interest?" "Do I tend to think about some things more than others?" Consider: "If I had only six months to live and I knew I couldn't fail, what's the one thing I would most intently want to do?" When you go into a bookstore, do you gravitate to one section or another? That can be an important clue.

A funny thing might happen as you begin to consider these things: you might hear a little voice inside that isn't very nice, trying to talk you away from your dream.

How to Avoid Self-Sabotage

The conscious and subconscious minds are like a "judge" and a "robot," respectively. It would seem natural that the judge (conscious mind) would control the robot (subconscious)—but the reverse is usually true: the robot is in control most of the time, except when occasionally, the judge grabs hold of the situation in a conscious manner.

The robot forgets nothing. Think of it as working like a balance scale. The positives are on one side, and the negatives are on the other. You are moving in the direction of your goals on one side of the scale and away from them on the other side. The rule is you can never take something off the scale; you can only add. So, if you add a new negative, it cannot be removed. You can counter only by adding a new positive. This is because your subconscious mind is so powerful. It remembers virtually everything you have ever experienced. However, it most readily accesses the most heavily weighted and recent experiences.

With goals, you may start with the scale heavily weighted in the wrong direction. Take quitting smoking as an example. You are offered a cigarette and your subconscious says, *Sure go ahead and take it. You're a smoker.* But if you write daily positively affirming, "I am a nonsmoker," eventually your subconscious will say, *You don't want that. You are not a smoker.*

The biggest threat to the fruition of our goals is ourselves. Remember Brian Tracy's lesson: "If it's to be, it's up to me." When we don't reprogram the robot, it will relentlessly set us up to keep doing the same old thing, good or bad!

Early in my tenure as CEO of MacDermid, I established a goal of creating one of the world's great industrial companies. Talk about dreaming! We were a small company surrounded by many large companies in our industry and even larger ones in other industries. The risk of setting a goal that big is you don't ever start because your subconscious mind says to you, *Don't be stupid; that's impossible.* As a result, you never start moving in that direction. Read on to understand how to make stretch goals realizable.

We are the ones who make things happen, change the robot, teach it the way we want it to think and perceive, and we alone are the ones who stand in our way. When we have negative self-image, every hour spent dwelling on negative thoughts or negative past feelings reinforces the robot's weight of evidence in support of our negative self-image. Every time you do something that moves you away from your goals, it becomes even harder to reach them.

Writing your goals is a primary way to overcome momentum in the wrong direction. It is a surefire cure for depression. Instead of dwelling on what takes us down, affirming the positive will convince us that there is hope, and the feelings from focusing on the positive will give a boost.

By the thoughts we choose to think, we are reprogramming our self-image either to work for us or against us, every moment of every day. Since our robot has no judgment function, it strives to meet whatever objectives and goals we set, whether positive or negative, true or false, right or wrong, good or bad.

My Robot by Denis Waitley

I have a little robot that goes around with me.
I tell him what I'm thinking, I tell him what I see.
I tell my little robot all my hopes and fears.
He listens and remembers all my joys and tears.
At first, my little robot followed my command—
But after years of training, he's gotten out of hand.
He doesn't care about what's right or wrong or what
  is false or true
No matter what I try now, he tells me what to do.

Behavioral scientists agree that our subconscious robot cannot tell the difference between real experiences and vivid imaginations. It stores emotional fantasies as realities. As a result, our minds are full of "Easter bunnies, the world is flat-isms"—perceived realities that simply are not real. Many of our everyday decisions are based upon information about ourselves that has been stored as truth but is just a figment of our imagination.

A key to change self-image is imagination. What you see in your mind's eye is what you get. The key is not reality, but your perception of it. A compelling example of this phenomenon happened during the Vietnam War. To stay sane and pass time, prisoners of war came up with activities to occupy their minds. In the famous Hanoi Hilton (Hỏa Lò Prison), the POWs came up with a code similar to Morse code that they tapped on the wall to communicate. They became so proficient at tapping, one Spanish-speaking inmate taught several fellow POWs to speak Spanish fluently by tapping on the wall. Some also played imaginary games of sport. Others played imaginary instruments. One group fashioned "guitars" out of sticks and taught each other to play chords on imaginary strings. Another POW played a full (imaginary) round of golf every day. He was a prisoner for seven years. Within a week of his release, he played in the New Orleans Open and shot a seventy-four, not having played a physical game in more than seven years!

The real core of the extraordinary ability of our brains to utilize imagination to turn it into real action and behavior is brain *plasticity*—our brain's capacity to constantly change itself, learn new things, and create new habits. It is what experts rely on to deeply think about their domain and become further experts. We will discuss brain plasticity and becoming an expert in chapter 5.

It's crucial that your goals be credible to you. In his book *Flow: The Psychology of Optimal Experience,* Dr. Mihaly

Csikszentmihalyi calls these types of goals *intrinsic*. In his book, *Maximum Achievement: Strategies and Skills That Will Unlock Your Hidden Powers to Succeed,* Brian Tracy writes: "Because belief is the catalyst that activates your mental powers, it is important that your goals be realistic, especially at first."[3]

Set subgoals that you can get your mind around. The subconscious mind will take them seriously. They supply motivation. Tracy suggests we write our goals daily in the form of positive affirmations. At first, rewriting goals every day may seem like overkill. Rewriting exactly the same words every day? As an inherently shy person especially in group settings, I used daily writings to work though my anxiety in social interactions. The first time I wrote, "I am comfortable in social situations," my negative self-talking mind answered, *Who are you kidding? You are scared to death of walking into a room full of people.* This is because I have given my subconscious lots of supporting data that formed such beliefs about who I am and how I act.

Our subconscious mind cannot tell the difference between real and vividly imagined experiences. Therefore, if we write our goals and subgoals in the form of positive affirmations, we can reprogram our mind to rewrite our future experiences as if they were already accomplished. After enough mental programming, if my subconscious mind sees me avoiding a personal interaction that could be uncomfortable, it says to my conscious mind, *Hey, why are you avoiding that person? She could be helpful to you. After all, you are a good people person.* Eventually I overcame my shyness in group settings. I didn't end up easily gravitating to these situations, but I learned to be effective when it mattered to me. Some people

---

3   Tracy, Brian. *Maximum Achievement: Strategies and Skills That Will Unlock Your Hidden Powers to Succeed.* New York, NY: Simon & Schuster, 1995.

who only know me professionally are shocked to learn I am a loner by nature.

After sufficient reprogramming, when faced with a fork in the road, your subconscious automatically points you in the direction in support of your larger, broader goals. This is why I suggest starting with a goal of writing goals. Something like, "I write my goals every day." If days go by and you don't write your goals, you will get a kick in the butt from your subconscious: *Hey, get your butt in gear and write your goals.* You won't even realize it is happening.

Imagine my starting point as MacDermid's CEO. "Congratulations, you are CEO of a company with profits of $8 million a year and had not grown earnings appreciably in five years." Our competitors were multibillion-dollar enterprises, like DuPont. Much of the business was under pressure. The U.S. automotive business was getting crushed by the Japanese, where we had no business. Automotive design styles were changing with chrome, our main offering, being replaced by solid colors where we did not have a product offering. Our electronics customers were consolidating and trying to commoditize our products. And, by the way, we were in the middle of a recession. The share price had been stagnant in the low twenties. So what is the first thing we did? We set a goal of $100 a share! Honestly, I had no idea how we were going to quadruple our share price. But I knew from my recent studying of success principles that unless I looked to make a real stretch, we would stay on a path of mediocrity.

At a certain point I came to understand the dynamic described above that can result in dramatic improvement potential, and it had a huge impact on me. I realized that if, in fact, I had hundreds or even thousands times potential to improve, what did the starting point really matter? Even though my past was checkered with failure, I knew I possessed some budding gifts through sports and my experience with Leever Brothers. I knew that through my passion, humility, and empathy for my fellow man, I could connect with my colleagues one-on-one in an uncommon way. If I could take these gifts and concentrate on improving the skills I would need in business—which contributed to the principles I now call The Formula—there was real hope for me.

> *"What man actually needs is not a tensionless state but rather the striving and struggling for some goal worthy of him."*
>
> —VIKTOR FRANKL

My Subgoals Toward My Big Dream

Dreaming big—*waaaaay* big—is good. It's the fire that gets us through cold nights of the soul. Just keep in mind we shouldn't try to eat the whale in one bite. Do not confuse your ultimate goal with immediate goals.

To make progress toward the ultimate, you need to craft smaller, more easily attainable goals, and then use them as you would stepping-stones to a high peak. Want to win an Academy Award? Awesome goal, but starting with the goal of taking an acting class might be necessary to trigger the neurochemicals that motivate you to start on your journey. After establishing a stretch, overarching goal, we break it down into more realistic, shorter-term subgoals. Set your bar at the right heights, and progressively, you manage to jump higher. Set it too high, however, and you risk failure. You become a casualty of stress. The key is to access the neurochemicals that excite and focus us, but not trigger stress-producing chemicals that immobilize us.

Brian Tracy has written widely about the right and wrong ways to set and reset goals. He says that goals that are set correctly force you to stretch without making you feel overwhelmed. He suggests starting with small goals, and as you gain experience and confidence with goal setting, you can take on goals with more daunting odds.

Using Tracy's advice, I set my goals and then expanded the affirmations so they would become tasks I could handle but that, when put together, would make up the tapestry of my larger overarching goal. Here they are as I'd written them:

Business: I am CEO of one of the world's greatest industrial enterprises.

- *I constantly show by example the value of serving—that aiding others in self-improvement leads to sustainable competitive advantage.*
- *MacDermid is growing by 25 percent a year.*
- *We acquire two companies over $10 million in sales, every year.*
- *We launch five new products with sales over $1 million first year, each year.*
- *I emphasize HR issues consuming half my time.*

Husband: I am an affectionate partner.

- *I show my affection often. I am supportive, understanding, loving, and make sacrifices often to meet my wife's needs.*
- *I am upbeat and happy; we laugh a lot.*

Father: I am a loving and supportive parent.

- *I make frequent deposits into Skip's emotional bank account.*
- *I am understanding of his trials.*
- *I listen to him.*
- *I show him by example the way to a happy, fulfilling life.*
- *I teach him the value of serving others.*

Self-improvement: I will learn something new every day and be smarter by the end of the day than when it started.

- *I read two nonfiction, business-strategy, organizational-development, psychology, or biographies per month.*
- *I study five mornings a week for thirty-five to forty-five minutes.*
- *I attend at least two self-improvement seminars a year.*
- *I write down my goals every day.*
- *I push the limits of personal growth and development.*

Health and fitness: I have achieved an outstanding level of health and fitness.

- *I exercise at least three to four days a week.*
- *My diet is excellent.*
- *My weight is below 175.*
- *I have achieved shape equal to when I was an athlete.*
- *I can ride my bike for one hour at twenty-one miles per hour.*

In many ways, my subgoals are measurable and specific enough to help me reflect on my behaviors and actions, and take inventory of what I have accomplished and what I need to work on.

What was the result of years of religiously writing my goals and personal affirmations and of dreaming big? I must admit looking back, if you were to judge me literally, the results are mixed. I am not sure I achieved any of the categories of goals 100 percent. I have no doubt, however, that I was far more successful in all areas than I would have been without these goals.

As mentioned at the beginning of this chapter, just as goal setting is vital to The Formula, so passion is vital to goal setting. Why? Because the mind seizes upon a passionately felt or passionately imagined goal more powerfully than some other goal about which you feel blasé. In goal setting, passion gives you what amounts to a passkey to the innermost recesses of your mind. You can find the prospect of your eating ice cream pleasant and attractive. Or you can burn with desire to eat it. You can want it so much that you can taste it in your mouth and feel its coolness on your tongue.

The difference matters. The more powerfully you feel the need, the easier and faster you will reach your goal. In setting goals, use passion as your guide: make your most important goals the ones you feel most passionately about. Next, we will discuss exactly how to ignite that passion and keep it burning for life.

CHAPTER 4

PRINCIPLE 4:
Summon Your Passion

When doing what we most love transforms into the
best possible version of ourselves and that version hints
at even greater future possibilities, the urge to explore
those possibilities becomes feverish compulsion.
Intrinsic motivation goes through the roof.

—STEVEN KOTLER, *RISE OF SUPERMAN*

'm a huge believer in the concept of passion. To me, Mac-Dermid was never an intellectual exercise. When somebody didn't follow the direction or wouldn't get on board, I perceived it as stealing a piece of our success. I fundamentally believe in certain principles. If I feel that somebody is working against my principles—which, importantly, is very different from having a disagreement—I get really pissed off. Passion is what it takes to get yourself excited as well as the people around you to work on something bigger than you. Passion is energizing, powerful, and fun! MacDermid and my passion for our excellence was not just fun for me; it was fun for everyone involved, from the highest to the lowest ranked colleagues.

What if you find yourself in a situation where you just can't find passion? There are two main reasons this happens:

you are in the wrong place with the wrong people in the wrong situation and/or you are unaligned with your true calling.

The first—wrong place, wrong everything—can happen for a person who considers himself or herself principled but discovers he or she is working with management or owners who are not. The similar can happen for a person who is senior enough in the company to have enough power to make cultural changes but is lambasted or hassled for it. There are too many headaches to have passion or at least sustain it.

The second—the unaligned person—is apparent in a person who gets a job that just doesn't fit their interests. This is probably not the environment for this person to practice "being yourself." It creates great stress to try to be someone you are not. Having said that, there are techniques to overcome limitations that may be getting in the way of passion. For example, let's say you are a real sports fanatic and want to make a career in the sports business. You get an entry-level position. You have lots of reason to be passionate. But the position isn't fun and doesn't play to your strength. Can you still find passion? You bet. It is all about mental programming to both increase your capabilities in areas in which you might not be as strong and position yourself to get into areas that are more aligned with you. Twice in my career I worked for virtually free just to get in the door. This includes my current gig working as Operating Partner for a private equity fund. I worked for them part time for a year with zero compensation while they were getting to understand my capability and raising a new fund. Now I am having a blast doing exactly what I love to do, and I am being richly compensated. I just had to make a little investment of time to solidify the opportunity.

How else is passion exhibited? Some of the elements of passion are part of the definition of an entrepreneur, someone who will not accept failure as an option. When entrepreneurs face a difficult challenge they persevere. Thomas Edison was asked if he was disappointed that he had not solved the technical issues surrounding the invention of the nickel-iron battery after literately thousands of experiments. In *Edison: His Life and Inventions*, Edison's long-time associate Walter S. Mallory tells the anecdote:

> *In view of this immense amount of thought and labor, my sympathy got the better of my judgment, and I said: "Isn't it a shame that with the tremendous amount of work you have done you haven't been able to get any results?" Edison turned on me like a flash, and with a smile replied: "Results! Why, man, I have gotten a lot of results! I know several thousand things that won't work."*[4]

Entrepreneurs do not recognize constraints, especially resource constraints. It is how small biotech companies with relatively miniscule resources continually out-innovate big pharma. At MacDermid we competed against DuPont, Dow, and other huge companies. Most observers would've looked at the relative financial resources and advised us to give up. Yet we continuously beat them in technology and in the marketplace.

As I reflect back on my darkest days, I feel real empathy for others, especially young people who may be in a dark place like I was and feel like there is no way out. No one wants to be depressed. No one wants to feel stupid. No one wants to be immobilized by anxiety. Getting from not being able to get out of bed to feeling the euphoria of being in flow is a long jump. I am not suggesting you get there in one day or in one step;

---

4   Martin, Thomas Commerford, and Frank Lewis Dyer. *Edison: His Life and Inventions*. New York, NY: Harper & Brothers, 1910.

I am saying there is a process that is proven and, if followed, it will take you to heights normal people can't imagine. And it is critical to understand *there are no losers* in this process. Embarking on this process will give you positive mental and physiological rewards almost from day one. Yes, getting to where I am, where you operate in flow most of the time, will take some time and significant mental programming. But just getting started will feel good. It is critical to remember it's about the journey not the destination. The simple pursuit of worthwhile goals is the key. In fact, the easier the process, the less you will get out of it. Our mind and bodies find utility in struggle.

How to Get Your Passion in Flow

In the last chapter, I gave you the bare science about the natural aids our body chemistry is able to drum up to help us stay disciplined, excited, and focused on our goal of gaining expertise. These aids are chemical compositions, powerful ones! Fortunately for us, these pharmacological cocktails are entirely naturally occurring and manufactured by our body.

Recently science has shown us that certain brain chemicals are produced and utilized when these circuits are being formed and optimized. Whereas there are dozens of neurochemicals, and perhaps more undiscovered, we will focus on the most important ones. As our nervous system secretes these chemicals, our neurons are either activated or deactivated with extremely precise timing. Our neurons fire and networks connect at precisely the exact moment to accomplish the task at hand. The more we practice deliberately, the better "tuned" our circuits become. An expert brain releases dopamine, endorphins, anandamide, and serotonin. Together these neurochemicals can provide a very powerful cocktail of world-class performance. Here are examples of the neuro-chemicals that play an important role in shaping our daily lives:

- Dopamine serves two physiological functions. The first is in goal setting. According to researchers at Duke University who published their findings in *The Journal of Neuroscience,* based on brain image studies, dopamine is released by the brain when we contemplate the completion of a project. Goal visualization releases dopamine. Secondly, science has demonstrated that dopamine is released whenever we take a risk or try something novel or exploratory that is outside our comfort zone. It helps us focus and increases our attention and pattern recognition. Dopamine is a very powerful "feel good" chemical. Therefore, it gives us a biological reinforcement to repeat the things that caused dopamine to be released in the first place. Dopamine reinforces a reward system for pursuing goals. Emotionally we experience dopamine as excitement, engagement, and creativity.

- Endorphins' principle function is to relieve pain and produce a feeling of euphoria. Endorphins are our body's natural opioids, or naturally occurring morphine. It is ironic that we have a national epidemic of synthetic opioid addiction when we have the same basic chemical *safely* and *naturally* available in our nervous system. We can get high anytime we want just by getting in flow. Runner's high may be related to the release of endorphins.

- The name anandamide is taken from the Sanskrit word *Amanda,* which means joy, bliss, and delight. Anandamide is a naturally occurring cannabinoid, making it our brain's natural marijuana. It reduces anxiety and aids memory consolidation, the process where things get transferred from short-term memory to long-term memory.

- Serotonin is our biological antidepressant. This neurochemical helps us stay positive throughout struggle. It is the natural Zoloft in our brain.

These neurochemicals are powerful alone, but in unison, they form an amazing cocktail of performance, multiplying our capabilities many times over. In fact, pursuing life with this cocktail present generates positive feelings. When these natural "drugs" are present, we don't need artificial ones. It is important to understand that, over the millions of years of our evolution, our bodies have adapted to create a balance of these neurochemicals. Anytime we take synthetic pharmaceuticals, prescribed or otherwise, we risk affecting this balance. I am not saying we should never take drugs like antidepressants. There may be folks who have no choice. But for the vast majority of us, there is more risk than reward.

These natural cocktails don't just show up. We have to create the mental and physical environments where they can be released by our nervous system. This is how I cured my depression.

The state when this cocktail emerges is termed "flow," first described by researcher Dr. Mihaly Csikszentmihalyi, who wrote the seminal book *Flow: The Psychology of Optimal Experience.* He writes, "In the Flow state people are so involved in an activity that nothing else seems to matter; the experience itself is so enjoyable that people will do it even at great cost, for the sheer sake of doing it."[5]

Since *Flow* was published twenty-five years ago, its research has been followed by an entire subsection of psychology. Recently Steven Kotler and Jamie Wheal released *The*

---

5   Csikszentmihalyi, Mihaly. *Flow: The Psychology of Optimal Experience.* New York, NY: Harper Perennial Modern Classics, 2008.

Rise of Superman: Decoding the Science of Ultimate Human Performance, as well as *Stealing Fire: How Silicon Valley, the Navy Seals, and Maverick Scientists Are Revolutionizing the Way We Live and Work.* They are definitely worth reading as they update the latest thinking on flow.

Professor Csikszentmihalyi and his colleagues developed a research procedure called the Experience Sampling Method (ESM). In this procedure, individuals wear an electronic pager that prompts them to write what they are feeling every time the pager signals, about eight times a day. Ultimately, Csikszentmihalyi and his colleagues collected more than a hundred thousand cross sections from different parts of the world.

Effectively the cocktail of neurochemicals described earlier works in concert to place your brain in a super-receptive state where the very act of thinking about moving your life in a positive direction causes joyous feelings. The state of flow is how world-class performers can stay focused for the ten or more years it takes to achieve their goal.

Flow must be intrinsic. Csikszentmihalyi describes how folks often give up on learning after they leave school. That is because all the school years learning was extrinsic, effectively forced upon them. Instead, he suggests we develop an intrinsic drive so that knowledge is something we want, not something forced upon us. He says:

Rather the goal is to understand what is going on around one, to develop a personally meaningful sense of what one's experience is all about. From that will come the profound joy of a thinker, like that experienced by the disciples of Socrates that Plato describes in The Philebus, *"The young man who has drunk for the first time from that spring is as happy as if he had found a treasure of wisdom; he is positively enraptured. He will pick up any discourse, draw all its ideas together to make them into one, then take them apart and pull them to pieces. He will puzzle first himself, then others, badger whoever comes near him, old and young, sparing not even his parents, nor anyone who is willing to listen . . ."* The quotation is about twenty-four centuries old, but a contemporary observer could not describe more vividly what happens when a person first discovers the flow of the mind.[6]

The results of harnessing flow lead to truly remarkable results in all walks of life. The Defense Advanced Research Projects Agency (DARPA) found that military snipers trained in a state of flow learned 230 percent faster than normal.[7] McKinsey researchers found executives were five times as productive while in flow.[8] We all know about athletes in the zone, or flow, who have incredible performances. In *The Formula,* we care most about how we can use the principles to learn faster and achieve more over time. Clearly harnessing the cocktail of neurochemicals will help us get there more quickly and will keep us motivated through the many hours required to build world-class mental representations. Csikszentmihalyi's research reported, "When we choose a goal and invest ourselves in it to the limits of our concentration,

6 Csikszentmihalyi, Mihaly. *Flow: The Psychology of Optimal Experience.* New York, NY: Harper Perennial Modern Classics, 2008.

7 Mindset 4 Progress. "How to learn 230% faster?" Mindset4Progress. com. December 27, 2017. Accessed August 20, 2018. mindset4progress. com/2017/12/27/how-to-learn-230x-faster/.

8 Cranston, Suzie, and Scott Keller. "Increasing the Meaning Quotient of Work." McKinsey and Company. Accessed August 20, 2018. www.mckinsey. com/business-functions/organization/our-insights/increasing-the-meaning-quotient-of-work.

whatever we do will be enjoyable. And once we have tasted this joy, we will redouble our efforts to taste it again; this is the way the self grows."[9]

For goals to be most effective, they need to be intrinsic, meaning they need to be of our choosing . . . for ourselves. To the extent goals are for others, they won't work. All they do is create needless stress. The key to goals is not the achievement, or "the destination," but instead, the idea is to focus on the process, or the "journey."

Csikszentmihalyi describes "intrinsic" as *autotelic,* which is derived from Greek words that mean *self* and *goal,* as opposed to "extrinsic," or *exotellic,* which are those activities done for external purposes. Csikszentmihalyi writes about how his research demonstrated that the world is full of folks who suddenly wake up at middle age with all the trappings of success, nice homes, fancy cars, and an Ivy League education but are deeply unhappy. They have gone through life hoping that by changing their external situation they would find happiness. In fact, focusing on our external environment is going about life all wrong. The way to achieve flow is to follow the basic structure of finding something, no matter how small, that you care about (passion), and follow the flow process: a) set a goal and as many subgoals as you can making sure that the subgoals are believable and achievable, but contain some amount of stretch, b) make sure goals are measurable, c) focus on the immediate subgoals, and d) treat your goals like steps on a staircase. Reach one and set a new one slightly higher, and repeat.

It is especially important that we avoid excessive passivity, which is in many ways the opposite of flow. It is the state

---

9   Csikszentmihalyi, Mihaly. *Flow: The Psychology of Optimal Experience.* New York, NY: Harper Perennial Modern Classics, 2008.

that so often drags us into depression and despair. Passivity occurs when we are not challenged. Effectively, our brains go into rest mode. Think in terms of watching TV, attending sporting events, and playing video games. They may stimulate our emotions, but they don't stimulate our brains. Of course, there is nothing wrong with switching off occasionally. We should just recognize that when we do, we are not producing the feel-good chemicals and are in a state of nothingness that does nothing positive for us. Professor Csikszentmihalyi refers to this state as apathy. He says:

> *One of the most ironic paradoxes of our time is the great availability of leisure that somehow fails to be translated into enjoyment. Compared to people living only a few generations ago we have enormously greater opportunities to have a good time, yet there is no indication that we actually enjoy life more than our ancestors did. Opportunities alone are not enough. We also need the skills to make use of them. And we need to know how to control consciousness—a skill that most people have not learned to cultivate. Surrounded by an astounding panoply of recreational gadgets and leisure choices, most of us go on being bored and vaguely frustrated.*[10]

Remember the comfort zone of the fleas in the bottle discussed in chapter 3? When we condition ourselves to adopt a mindset that is apathetic, we limit our potential and lose our passion for what we know we can inherently do and what we can become experts at—like jumping super high.

What Samuel Johnson so memorably said about one's

---

10 Csikszentmihalyi, Mihaly. *Flow: The Psychology of Optimal Experience.* New York, NY: Harper Perennial Modern Classics, 2008.

prospect of being hanged in a fortnight ("it concentrates his mind wonderfully") can be said equally of passion: focusing on what you feel most passionate about tends to force petty and less vital distractions from your attention. If you have a wandering mind or if, like me, you have a bit less left brain than others, summoning up passion can help keep your mind clear and focused. In the next chapter, we will discuss becoming a world-class expert. Passion that drives focus and clarity (flow) is vital to that journey.

Over the years, I have experimented with different methods to get me into the flow state. Earlier I shared with you my daily goal of writing my daily affirmations, but here I hope to inspire you with other ideas that have worked to help me tap into the passion and flow and, in my case, the concentration required to achieve what I set out to do.

1. **Morning goal setting.** As a starting point, I suggest you carve out fifteen minutes first thing in the morning. Get a cup of coffee or your preferred morning beverage and sit in a quiet place. Use those fifteen minutes to write in a journal. Establish one goal. My favorite is "I will spend fifteen minutes a day reflecting on my future." Another I like is "I write my goals daily." You will be amazed how after a few weeks of doing this you will feel better about yourself.

2. **Exercise.** Exercise is a powerful generator of helpful neurochemicals. Sometimes it is hard to start exercising if you aren't used to doing so. Keep in mind that any kind of exercise is helpful. An early morning brisk walk is very useful for getting you going when you first begin. Over time you can pick up the pace and enjoy a painless start to your day. I listen to nonfiction audiobooks as I take my easy morning run. This way I accomplish two tasks with one action.

3. **Read nonfiction.** The average person reads five books a year. People who make over $50,000 per year read twice as many books as people who make under $30,000. I read over fifty nonfiction books last year. Do you think there will be a difference between my mental representations and that of a person who reads five books? Reading or listening to interesting nonfiction books will activate the parts of your brain that you want to grow.

Passion is the rocket fuel to propel us toward our dreams. Next, you will learn about directing your passion.

CHAPTER 5

PRINCIPLE 5:
Become World Class

An investment in knowledge pays the best interest.

—Benjamin Franklin

I t's unlikely we will ever experience success at the levels we aspire to without developing expert or even world-class capabilities. There are many smart, capable folks out there. For us to differentiate ourselves from the competition, we need to develop skillfulness in our endeavors. I am a big believer in nurture over nature, of tenacity over talent, because nurture and tenacity imply time and energy and focus spent on developing an aptitude for a chosen domain. That investment is what creates experts.

At a certain point in my growth, I started to believe in the power of human compounding in our brain, that building upon each learning would compound the learning over time. I didn't understand the science then, but as I was attending the self-help seminars and reading the likes of Brian Tracy, all these gurus emphasized the concept that what we dwell on grows. The more I studied and concentrated on these issues, I could see myself developing an increased awareness of business concepts.

In this chapter, you will learn about the practice and science behind becoming world class. Really world class. I define "world class" as a unique capability or understanding that surpasses others that work in a field and may have significant expertise. Many world-class people are accused of lacking work-life balance. Yes, it's true: if you want to achieve genuine differentiation, you can't do what everyone else does. I used to think I had an unhealthy work-life balance. After reading dozens of biographies of world-class people such as Benjamin Franklin, Winston Churchill, Albert Einstein, J. D. Rockefeller, Steve Jobs, Leonardo Da Vinci, Sam Walton, and many others, I came to realize that, in some way or another, they were all so extremely focused that some observers considered their lifestyles unbalanced. The passion and focus they exhibited on one big dream are essential ingredients in The Formula, so let's now dive into the science of passion and focus.

What we can now see and therefore prove with imaging technology is that neurons are our mind and body's communication mechanism. For any thought, feeling, or action to occur, a series of neurons must fire. Our nervous system has hundreds of billions of neurons that make hundreds of trillions of connections called synapses. A typical neuron can reset itself in about five microseconds, or about 200 times a second. Furthermore, these neurons work in parallel. Two hundred times per second, multiplied by billions of simultaneous firings leads to an almost unimaginable capacity.

The processing speed of our brain is estimated to measure in the billion bits per second. In 2016 researchers from the Salk Institute for Biological Sciences, the renowned California-based research institution, discovered new ways to measure brain capacity. Their researchers now estimate the brain has the storage capacity of 1 petabyte, or 1,024 terabytes, one quadrillion bytes. To put that in context, 1 petabyte is as much as the contents of the entire World Wide Web.[11]

The point here is that capacity is not anyone's limiting factor. We possess incredible, almost unimaginable brainpower. This capacity is largely untapped in most of us. Literally, we can accomplish virtually anything if we put our mind to it.

So let's agree that capacity is not the issue in maximizing human potential. The issue is *access* to our innate capacity. The capacity just described is the speed of our subconscious mind. Our conscious mind, on the other hand, is very slow, as it is far too limited in capacity. It is estimated that our conscious mind operates at 40 bits of information per second, and we know our subconscious operates at millions or even billions of bits per second. Forty bits compared to millions? What's going on here? The key is in how our conscious and subconscious minds process information. The conscious mind operates serially or one input at a time. The subconscious system operates in a parallel manner, processing multiple inputs simultaneously. Our subconscious mind is made up of hundreds of trillions of synapses. Yes, our capacity is mind-boggling. As you will learn next, exactly how fast our neurons "talk" is a matter of how we prepare them.

In chapter 3, I introduced the judge and the robot in describing our conscious and subconscious minds as they relate to our comfort zone and avoiding incrementalism. Here we are going a little deeper as we discuss the relative difference in the basic processing between our "two selves."

Our neurons and synapses create networks that become interconnected. These networks can run in length from our

---

11 Salk. January 20, 2016. "Memory Capacity Is Ten Times More Than Previously Thought." *Salk Institute News.* January 20, 2016. Accessed August 20, 2018. https://www.salk.edu/news-release/memory-capacity-of-brain-is-10-times-more-than-previously-thought/.

central nervous system all the way to the remote reaches of our limbs. These networks are not fixed, nor is the speed of the connections between them constant. If we are slow to access our capacity, it doesn't matter how much capacity we have, as the queue is too long.

Our nervous system, including our brain, is malleable, changeable, or plastic, as science calls it. Plasticity, or change-ability, is the key to understanding how we access our tremendous capacity. Effectively, plasticity describes our brain's ability to adapt and change over time. Circuits are formed and neurons are added, pruned, and rearranged such that over a long period in the right circumstances, we become a completely new version of ourselves.

We are born with few of our circuits formed or interconnected. We do not start life with sophisticated higher order human mental processing. We are born with the potential to create networks that lead to achieving this higher order thinking. Every time we fire one or a series of neurons in a certain manner, networks begin to be created. Our circuits are rudimentary and slow operating at first—think of a baby learning to walk or talk. Little by little, these networks become faster and more effective. With literally an unimaginable number of connections possible, we spend virtually our entire lives establishing networks and then perfecting them.

What is the difference between a world-class performer and others? An authority in the field of expertise is Dr. K. Anders Ericsson of the University of Florida. His recent book *Peak: Secrets from the New Science of Expertise,* coauthored by Robert Pool, is a must-read if you want to understand the subject of expertise. In *Peak,* the authors describe the acquisition of expertise and answer the question, "What is required to attain world-class status?"

What makes a Roger Federer, Yo-Yo Ma, or Warren

Buffett able to outperform the average person? Are these people naturally gifted, or is there some other reason? Dr. Ericsson suggests that the mental representations of world-class performers are more developed due to years of a certain type of practice. Not just any type of practice will do. More to come on this topic, but first a little background.

Think, for example, of someone tossing a toddler a tennis ball. Of course the toddler comes nowhere close to catching it. That is because the child's conscious processing is far too slow to react real time. Even if the ball is tossed from a very close distance *very* slowly, when the child tries to catch a ball the first few times, his mind cannot identify the ball, calculate where it is going, move his hand, and close his fingers around it to catch it in the time allowed. Eventually, if the child is like most of us, he'll get pretty good at catching the tennis ball tossed in his direction from close distance. If he's like some of us, with practice, he can even handle a tennis ball being served to him in a tennis match.

Is the amateur tennis player more gifted than a non-tennis player trying to "see" a serve for the first time? And how about professionals? Some touring pros are better at a single surface. Some are clay court specialists, grass specialists, or hard court specialists. This is because it is relatively easier to develop the mental representations in a single surface than in multiple ones—the ball bounces slightly differently, spin affects it differently, and speed of play is different. But to win on all surfaces, like Roger Federer, is far more challenging and requires many more hours building the circuits to be proficient.

Do we really think Yo-Yo Ma came out of the womb playing the cello to rapt audiences at Carnegie Hall? It is impossible for untrained fingers to coax the sounds out of instruments using the thought process of the conscious mind, thinking about each finger placement one by one, while directing the bow and remembering the notes that follow. Through brain imaging, scientists can see unique physiological characteristics of string professionals' brains. The part of the brain that operates the fingers of the left hand is much more pronounced in these people. This phenomenon is called physiological adaptation. The brain physically adapts to the effort of world-class string players over time.

Consider this financial problem: What is the impact on intrinsic value of the terminal value versus perpetuity method? A person untrained in finance would have a very difficult time answering that question. A non-business person wouldn't even understand the question. In fact, I bet if you ask 99 percent of businesspeople this question, even they would struggle. Ask Warren Buffett, and he'd have an instant answer. In fact, this is a very complex problem that you can't begin to answer without a lot of training and deep thought. Buffett has spent a lifetime immersed in the fields of finance and economics. He can get to the crux of a financial issue in milliseconds, and then *begin* thinking about it. Most people don't even get to his starting point. This process is advanced mental representations.

As we challenge our neuronal system over and over, we fire our neurons and create these networks, or mental representations. Information is taken into our conscious processing center and over time is moved to our subconscious processing system. Ultimately, this is what differentiates us as humans. The subconscious processing system creates mental pictures that become available to us to create patterns that can be used to solve problems or to conduct highly complex physical or mental actions. These mental representations predict, in real time, what we are about to see and do.

The more automatic our predictions become the less conscious brainpower is required to perform the action and the faster we can access these mental representations. Think of the efforts of a toddler learning to speak—not exactly fluent. The difference between a toddler and a ten-year-old is better mental representations developed over the intervening years through constant use of the circuits that control verbal processing. The difference between the ten-year-old and a high school debate participant? You guessed it, more mental representations. And so it goes, all the way up the ladder.

What Is Required to Attain World-Class Status?

The physical mechanism of developing these neuronal circuits that create mental representations is called *myelination*. Through recent advances in brain imaging, we can actually see our brains becoming more efficient. Imagine your neuronal connections as uninsulated wires, which are inherently inefficient as electricity dissipates from an uncontrolled environment. Add insulation and electricity is channeled to travel much more quickly and efficiently. In myelination, our neuronal connections are "insulated" a tiny bit at a time. As we fire our circuits, we insulate the neuronal connections, and they fire more quickly in a more automatic manner. How much more quickly? About 3,000 times more quickly for a world-class circuit compared to an untrained one. This is the reason a chess grand master can play many simultaneous matches . . . blindfolded! His or her processing speed and mental representations are developed over so many years that compared to non-grand masters these players are light-years faster and more accomplished.

Think of Olympic divers twisting and turning in a beautiful sequence that an untrained person can only dream about. Yet they can perform the dives over and over with near absolute precision, barely making a ripple as they enter the water.

This is possible because the neuronal networks that control the muscles necessary to perform the complex movements in the dive have become completely automatic. These are tasks no one could possibly come close to accomplishing mechanically using their slow conscious mind. Our conscious minds are far too slow to sequence: jump on the diving board, bring left hand over right shoulder, bend at the waist, look to the right to cause the first spin, and then continue this mechanical process for six or more maneuvers in the same dive. These are fully automatic processes being instructed to our mind at the rate of as much as billions of bits a second.

The problem with building these networks of mental representations through myelination is that it is painstakingly slow. The myelin sheath forms around our circuits in incredibly thin layers of myelin, wrap by wrap, insulating the nerve fibers. The complexity of the task of insulating perhaps hundreds of thousands of neural pathways for a single activity, such as recognizing the patterns of chess pieces on a board, takes years. So, does practice make perfect? No, practice makes myelin, and myelin makes perfect. Daniel Coyle describes this process very well in his book *The Talent Code: Greatness Isn't Born. It's Grown. Here's How.* I would highly recommend this book if you want a little deeper understanding of this subject.

Yes, it takes practice to become expert—huge amounts of it. In some domains, it takes ten years or more of daily practice. In my case, I believe my intense focus on the study of business and finance gave me unique and extremely valuable insights that were a major reason for my success.

As our circuits slowly develop, they get more and more efficient. At first after, say, a year of practice you become a little more efficient. Year by year, you compound the efficiency gains until it becomes possible for you to become thousands of times more efficient. In *Peak,* Ericsson and Pool describe what it takes to become world class. Importantly, not any kind of practice will do. It takes a certain type of practice to continue the path to become world class. This is called deliberate practice. "Deliberate" means effortful, focused on a challenge that is just outside your comfort zone, coupled with frequent feedback.

Performing an activity without deliberate practice is why so many weekend golfers never improve their handicap. A new golfer spends considerable time learning the game, practicing the different strokes to gain some amount of proficiency. Once the weekend golfer gets to an acceptable level, she stops practicing and just "plays golf." The result? Plateau. She never gets any better. To be world class, you can't just "play" golf; you have to practice deliberately, a lot. This is also why we reach a certain point as car drivers and never improve. If simply spending thousands of hours just doing one activity would lead to world class, we would all be Formula 1 drivers. In chapter 3, we discussed the subjects of comfort zone and homeostasis. We need to get outside of our comfort zone, break out of homeostasis, and that means utilizing the components of deliberate practice as I just described.

The impact of the science of becoming world class for The Formula is straightforward. If we really have the ability to be hundreds or even thousands times faster or better than we are at the start of our journey, does it really matter what the relative starting point is compared to our competition? It is not a matter of whether we can differentiate ourselves to achieve success—it is just a matter of organizing to do so—and here's the key: executing the plan. We know it can take ten years of deliberate practice to get there. Yes, indeed it is a marathon, not a sprint, which means that patience, stamina, and passion are required.

CHAPTER 6

PRINCIPLE 6:
Think Deeply

We cannot solve our problems with the same thinking we used when we created them.

—ALBERT EINSTEIN

In 2007 the boardrooms of Lehman Brothers, Merrill Lynch, Citigroup, and many other investment banks, hedge funds, and private equity funds were filled with some of the most elite, smartest, best-educated folks who were experiencing record years at their respective companies and earning the most money of their lives. They were all making assumptions about the future and virtually all were forecasting the continuation of economic prosperity. They were wrong.

In 2008 the global markets were hit with the worst financial crisis in a generation. Lehman went bankrupt, Merrill Lynch was sold in a fire sale, and Citigroup had to be bailed out by the government. Private equity funds that were fundraised in 2007, referred to as 2007 vintage funds, had the lowest returns in history. None of these "smartest guys in the room" saw the 2008 financial crisis coming. The effect was that people like you and me had to use our tax dollars to bail out all the large banks. How could so many "smart" ones be so wrong? They didn't think deeply.

Another one of our core principles in The Formula is thinking deeply—using your mind far beyond the easy answers and searching for an understanding that does not come to us intuitively. It means not jumping to quick conclusions. What is the science behind deep thinking? As amazing as our brain is, it is not perfect. Seminal work in how our brain functions was conducted by Nobel Laureate Daniel Kahneman and his frequent co-researcher Amos Tversky. Their research is described in Kahneman's book *Thinking, Fast and Slow*. They represent a fairly recent area of psychology called behavioral psychology that studies the decision process we utilize in real life. This is opposed to most psychology, which is more theoretical. In *Thinking, Fast and Slow*, Kahneman characterizes our brain as System 1 and System 2. System 1 is similar to my description of subconscious, and system 2 similar to my description of conscious discussed in chapters 3 and 5. So says Kahneman, "Statistics produce many observations that appear to beg for causal explanations but do not lend themselves to such explanations. Many facts of the world are due to chance, including accidents of sampling."[12]

Our brain is organized in layers of increasing hierarchy. When the brain encounters an input that is well wired from previous mental representations, it processes the information automatically without thinking at the lowest level of the hierarchy. This automaticity is what we mean by subconscious. As newer, less-recognized inputs arrive, they are kicked up the hierarchy for further processing. This can be repeated up to five layers or hierarchal levels in our brain. Each layer

---

12 Kahneman, Daniel, and Amos Tversky. *Thinking, Fast and Slow*. New York, NY: Farrar, Straus, and Giroux, 2013.

requires more thought or conscious processing. Each stage is slower and uses more energy.

Our brain is essentially lazy. It wants to use the least energy possible. Therefore, it will err by making decisions by intuition at a lower, speedy level. This is good and bad. At the default setting, our brain will access the prior mental representations and quickly and intuitively guide us. This is how we can drive a car without thinking. We can drive while carrying on a detailed conversation with the person seated next to us. However, when something unexpected happens in front of us, like a car swerving or a cat darting out between parked cars, we lose our ability to carry on the conversation as our attention is consumed by the events in front of us.

As powerful as our subconscious mind is, it can be fallible at the same time. If our subconscious is faced with something outside its comfort zone, it can send the issue up to our conscious mind for processing, but as we have learned, that is a relatively slow process. It can also rearrange the facts to fit an existing mental representation and essentially shortcut the processing. This process is called *heuristics*. Sometimes this is an expedient way to process things quickly or when the conscious mind is otherwise occupied. This is where the terms "rule of thumb" and "educated guess" come from. In life, we have no choice but to use mental shortcuts. The problem is, sometimes when our mind takes these shortcuts, it leaves out too many of the relevant facts and our conclusion becomes flawed or biased.

How Shortcuts Short-Circuit Our Abilities

There are many examples of heuristic biases, which even the world's most-known experts possess. One example is errors caused by small sample size. In *Thinking, Fast and Slow,* which I highly recommend, Kahneman describes a study of education.

In one such study, researchers surveyed 1,662 schools in Pennsylvania to determine what characteristics were common in the top-performing schools. They found that six of the top fifty were small schools, a far higher percentage than would have been indicated by pure statistics. This made sense. One might expect a smaller school with smaller class sizes and individual attention would be more effective. Based on this and other similar research, the Gates Foundation made a $1.7 billion investment in the creation of small schools. This was followed by other major charities and the U.S. Department of Education's small learning communities program.

The only problem was the findings were wrong. If the statisticians had asked about the worst schools, they would have found they too were smaller schools. What gives? What was ultimately determined is that the smaller schools are not more or less effective; they are just more variable. Behavioral science has shown us the fallacy in small sample sizes. We naturally tumble to flawed conclusions because they "make sense." It is difficult for our minds to be rigorous enough to ask the hard questions about the data; we just believe the story. To not simply believe the story is precisely what I mean by thinking deeply. It is just too easy to see a data point that supports your intuition and stop there. But it is what we naturally do.

Using The Formula, we stop so we can further process the data and ask ourselves if there might be different or additional data that could change our conclusion. In the case of the education research, asking, "Is this too easy of an answer? Did we ask if the sample size was statistically supportable?" would be in order.

Kahneman and Tversky reported on studies of experts, some of whom had graduate degrees in statistics. They found that experts undersized the sample size of their studies so overwhelmingly that the studies produced erroneous results. The experts just fell into the trap of taking shortcuts that intuitively made sense to them, even though the outcome of their study proved entirely wrong.

Two rounds of Nobel Prizes in economics have been erroneously awarded and pervasive market strategies are based on economic theories based on biased heuristics that were later proven wrong. Consider these three financial theories: capital asset pricing model (CAPM), the efficient market hypothesis (EMH), and the Black-Scholes-Merton model. In similar arguments, these theories argue that the market is rational and that prices always reflect all the known information and that it is impossible, in the long run, to achieve returns in excess of the returns for the market in general. There is a mathematic model that supports these theories. The only problem is that the theories and underlying models use the Gaussian distribution commonly known as the bell curve. The bell curve describes "normal distributions." It describes standard deviations. Using this calculation, one can predict with a fairly high degree of accuracy the deviation from the midpoint of a set of data.

Nassim Nicholas Taleb is the author of several books on the subject of fat-tailed or improbable events. His most well-known book is *The Black Swan: The Impact of the Highly Improbable*. His argument is that the bell curve, by its mathematical nature, is not appropriate to use in all situations, because it does not allow for highly improbable but important events. He used this example to describe the different ways to look at the impact from variation:

Let's play the following thought experiment. Assume you round up a thousand people randomly selected from the general public and have them stand next to each other in a stadium. . . . Imagine the heaviest person you can think of and add him to that sample. Assuming he weighs three times the average, between four hundred and five hundred pounds, he will rarely represent more than a very small fraction of the weight of the entire population (in this case, about a half a percent) . . . You can get even more aggressive. If you picked the heaviest biologically possible human on the planet (who yet can still be called a human), he would not represent more than, say, 0.6 percent of the total, a very negligible increase. Then, consider by comparison the net worth of the thousand people you lined up in the stadium. Add to them the wealthiest person to be found on the planet—say Bill Gates, the founder of Microsoft. Assume his net worth to be close to $80 billion—with the total capital of the others around a few million. How much of the total wealth would he represent? 99.9 percent?[13]

Can you imagine what the curve would look like in the Gates Foundation's large versus small school case? You can see clearly with this example that the bell curves math works fine in the first example, but utterly fails in the second. In the case of the stock market, it fails to be useful in forecasting because there are infrequent market crashes that have a huge impact on returns. However, they are so infrequent that there is no way to use a mathematical model to forecast them. So, what happens is the bell curve works most of the time, but

---

13 Taleb, Nassim Nicholas. *The Black Swan: The Impact of the Highly Improbable.* New York, NY: Random House, 2010.

not all of the time. Where the Nobel winners went wrong is they used too short a period to go back and test their models. If they had gone back far enough, they would have seen the math was not applicable for this purpose. They did not think deeply enough.

The amazing history of this argument concluded when two of the men behind the Black-Scholes-Merton model formed Long-Term Capital Management—one of the biggest hedge funds. The partners were so certain that their math was correct and so esteemed were their mathematical reputations, they raised billions of dollars and then borrowed billions more from many of Wall Street's most famous houses to bet on their mathematics. The result? In 1998 the hedge fund blew up in one of the largest failures in the history of Wall Street, a failure of one firm that almost brought down the entire financial system. The incredible story is chronicled in the book *When Genius Failed: The Rise and Fall of Long-Term Capital Management* by Roger Lowenstein. Yet Wall Street, even after being on the absolute brink of disaster, continued to make leveraged bets until the system did fail in 2008 and the government had to bail out Wall Street. Shameful. What went on here? Heuristics.

The Nobel winners and the market participants took mental shortcuts. Their math worked most of the time . . . until it didn't. One can prove almost any theory of the market if you get to choose the time period. Then the inevitable black swan event comes along and wipes you out. So, am I saying individuals received Nobel Prizes based on false models? Yup. Warren Buffett has been warning us about this for thirty years. How did he see it when the entire financial world did not?

First, he thought deeply. He used his conscious mind to probe deeply into these matters, thereby avoiding falling into the trap of heuristic shortcutting. He did not stop at the easy answer. And how about Buffett's mental representations? Buffett started studying the financial markets when he was ten years old. He devoted virtually every free moment to its pursuit. By devoting, at current count, seventy-five years to this pursuit, do you think he might have developed better mental models with which to analyze financial data? He became world class. His mental models are so advanced that, combined with thinking deeply, they result in an understanding few others can match.

There are many other heuristics that our mind uses to take shortcuts for the sake of efficiency. Some of the more important include the narrative bias and the confirmation bias. In the narrative bias, we use stories to make sense of the world. It is much easier to input a story into our subconscious than a bunch of facts. The only problem is our subconscious believes stories—whether or not they are true. Unless we interject our conscious mind to "think about" the issue, our subconscious mind will just accept the story as fact. The confirmation bias is even more perplexing. With this bias, we filter out inputs that go against our current beliefs and selectively take in the inputs that support our beliefs. That is why a political left leaner can listen to a report and a right leaner can listen to the identical report and each "hears" an entirely different message.

How to Minimize the Shortcut Trap

Yes, heuristics are real. Worse yet, we cannot avoid them. It's simply how we are physiologically wired. So what to do? There are two approaches to minimize the impact of heuristics. The first is to develop very deep mental representations in the areas that matter to us. By doing so, we can filter out the noise. My area of interest is business. By studying the subject deeply, I know to tune out when a prognosticator on a morning financial show starts talking about future trends in interest rates, currency, or commodity prices. I know it is simply impossible to forecast these things.

The second approach in avoiding heuristics is to recognize how prevalent they are. Then, when faced with a very important decision, we need to force ourselves to stop and engage our conscious mind. No quick, important decisions allowed. Think deeply when it matters.

Is it possible heuristics played a role in my development of The Formula? Frankly, yes, it's possible. I did not do a controlled study of a robust sample size that studied people who exhibited the same characteristics as my heroes. Would I have found that there are millions of passionate people who thought deeply, dreamed big and set goals, and were long-term oriented, but never made it? Perhaps. That is why I spent so much time on the science of thinking deeply, of goal setting and programming the brain, and of how to develop world-class capabilities. Provable scientific physiological mechanisms *are* at play here. Will they guarantee you success beyond your wildest dreams? Yes, I believe so. But, even if I am wrong, the worst that can happen is The Formula will lead you to live a lifelong journey that is healthy, motivating, energizing, and happy.

The principle of not jumping to conclusions or avoiding the easy, less-thoughtful answers is fundamental to The Formula. My experience has shown over and over that people do not carefully consider all of the alternatives when forming an opinion. I have long referred to this phenomenon as logical fallacy. Logical fallacy commonly occurs when one adds up facts and then processes those facts to draw a conclusion. Because one follows a factual, logical path, the mind assumes the conclusion must be correct. As far as the thought process goes, of course the conclusions must be accurate. The fallacy in the conclusion lies not from the facts considered, but by the facts not considered, that were left out of the analysis. For example, we spend billions of dollars forecasting things like economic demand, interest rates, inflation, oil prices, and the like. Did you know that the long-term track record of these forecasts is no better than random chance? Yet, we spend lots of time listening to these forecasters.

John Kenneth Galbraith, the noted economist, once said, "The only function of economic forecasts is to make astrology look respectable."[14] In the May 19, 2015 issue, *Business Insider* published the twelve worst predictions about the global economy that intelligent people ever produced. These are very interesting examples of smart people who completely miss the data points that would lead them to the correct conclusion. It's amazing in retrospect how wrong these famous prognosticators were. Take a look:

1. "Japan as Number One" was released by Harvard social scientist Ezra Vogel back in 1979. It was not an unpopular view at the time that the United States economy would soon be surpassed by prosperous Japan, but it looks pretty ridiculous now.

2. Irving Fisher, one of America's greatest ever economists, said in October 1929 that he believed equities had reached a "permanently high plateau." Less than two weeks later, stocks plunged and didn't reach the highs they fell from for twenty-five years.

3. In December 2007, Goldman Sachs chief investment strategist Abby Joseph Cohen made a Fisher-like prediction of her own. She suggested the S&P 500

---

14 Poston, Toby. "The Legacy of JK Galbraith." BBC News. April 30, 2006. Accessed August 20, 2018. news.bbc.co.uk/2/hi/business/4960280.stm.

would hit 1,675 by the end of 2008, a climb of 14 percent—it actually ended below 900.

4. Paul Samuelson, the first American to win the Nobel Prize in economics, said in 1961 that "the Soviet economy is proof that, contrary to what many skeptics had earlier believed, a socialist command economy can function and even thrive."

5. In 2010, billionaire entrepreneur Richard Branson issued a warning that "the next five years will see us face another crunch—the oil crunch," predicting a severe supply shortage. Five years later, the price of oil is actually lower than it was then.

6. James Glassman and Kevin Hassett's 1999 book *Dow 36,000* predicted that the Dow Jones stock index would more than triple in the years ahead. Even now, 18 years later, the index is only 21,000, still far short of 36,000.

7. Former Fed Chair Alan Greenspan warned in his 2007 book *The Age of Turbulence* that the world might need double-digit interest rates to control inflation in the near future. Rates have been near zero for the vast majority of the time since.

8. Joan Robinson, one of the 20th century's most prominent Keynesian economists, visited the Koreas in 1964 and said "as the North continues to develop and the South to degenerate, soon or later the curtain of lies must surely begin to tear."

9. Joseph Cassano, who ran insurer AIG's financial products division, had his own financial crisis howler. In August 2007, Cassano said he couldn't see AIG

"losing one dollar in any of those (credit derivative) transactions." AIG was bailed out in 2008.

10. Professor Ravi Batra wrote a book called *The Great Depression of 1990,* predicting global turmoil. It was a New York Times number-one bestseller in 1987, and Milton Friedman said he wouldn't "touch (the book) with a ten foot pole."1990 is more generally remembered as one of the beginning years of an extended global boom period.[15]

Another area that is susceptible to onerous conclusions is research. In 2015 the Open Science Collaboration, a group of more than 250 researchers, published the results of their attempt to reproduce 100 studies from three top journals in social and cognitive psychology. In a shocking result, they reported that more than 60 percent of the results could not be replicated. What's going on here?

There are two theories that help explain the result. First is the difference between correlation and causation. There is a huge difference. It is common that something is correlated but not causal. Consider this: in one famous example, a research study showed a strong, positive relationship between ice cream sales and crime. When sales went up, so did crime, and vice versa. Does this mean that buying ice cream *causes* crime? Or is there some other factor involved, such as weather or time? People purchase more ice cream in warmer months. People are also outside more in warmer months with their homes unattended for longer periods of time. If you incorrectly

---

15 Bird, Mike. "12 of the Worst Economic Predictions Ever Made by Highly Intelligent People." *Business Insider.* May 20, 2015. Accessed August 20, 2018. www.businessinsider.com/12-of-the-worst-predictions-about-the-global-economy-that-intelligent-people-have-ever-made-2015-5.

assume that ice cream causes crime, would you stop the sale of ice cream to combat crime? Yes, there is a correlation, but there clearly is not a causal relationship between ice cream and crime. You have to think deeply. This is a trap some of the studies fall into.

The second problem that may have caused poor replication of the studies is the "file drawer effect." Researchers have a natural tendency to look for confirmation of their hypotheses when conducting studies. As a result, they tend to publish the confirmatory findings and put the nonconfirmatory findings away in a file drawer. Therefore, reviewers and subsequent researchers do not have access to these data points. These are often highly trained scientists. The moral of the story is be skeptical and think deeply.

How Deep Thinking Helped Me in My Business

Part of our deep thinking at MacDermid involved our acquisition strategy. Under my leadership, we acquired thirty companies. Common wisdom would say you acquire a business and add it to your business, but this doesn't address nonessential costs in the form of overlaps. Our approach was to virtually completely eliminate nonessential costs. When you acquire a business, there are natural overlaps, two CEOs, two CFOs, two accounting departments, two HR departments, etc. Our target was always zero duplication. We didn't always get to zero, but we got very close. No one was doing this in those days. Today most famously 3G Capital has used this approach in their investments in Burger King and Anheuser-Busch and have been rewarded in billions of dollars in gain.

Using this strategy, the more businesses we acquired, the more profit we had available to acquire additional businesses. These higher profits from acquired companies also allowed us to spend even more on the customer-facing side. We increased investments such as R&D (research and development) to insure we had the best products, and we increased the investment in the field sales and technical infrastructure. All of this allowed us to materially, strategically mitigate the pressures on our business.

In our industrial business, we acquired two of the largest chemical automotive suppliers in Europe, thereby reducing the dependence the business had on the U.S. automotive business. Over the next several years, we grew our automotive business through acquisition by eight times, transforming the business from a niche U.S. player to a global powerhouse. We acquired new business areas in printing and oil and gas services to further spread the risk across multiple industries.

This was all part of thinking deeply for the long game. If you want to insure a sustainable enterprise for generations, you can't follow the herd. In electronic chemicals, we made a bet on new technology. Through a heavy investment in R&D, we positioned our electronic chemicals business as a "can't substitute" technology and set our price point as such. This was a huge bet because one of our largest competitors, Rohm and Haas (now DowDuPont), a huge chemical conglomerate, had caved in to the commoditization pressure and had begun lowering its prices.

In one of the scariest decisions of my career, we held firm on our prices and did not lower them to match Rohm and Haas. We immediately lost a couple of our largest customers. My bet was the customers would fail with the Rohm and Haas technology as their plants had been built around our technology. Effectively, the equipment used to produce products was special made around our technology. We bet it wouldn't work, or at least wouldn't work near as well, causing difficulties for the customers and driving them back to us. If

I had been wrong, our company would have gone bust. But, alas, within a year, we prevailed, the customer went bankrupt, and the industry structure survived. Effectively, the products that had been produced by that customer were moved to our customers, and we won.

These examples describe the importance of thinking deeply. Our logic was that if we accepted the proposed industry-pricing structure, we would be materially weakened, regardless of the circumstances. Therefore, we bet our technology would carry the day. If we had been wrong, Rohm and Haas would have gained huge market share at our expense. We felt it would be a hollow victory. It's tough to make up for lower prices with more volume.

Much later after the electronics chemical market had stabilized, the market was evidenced by fighting hard every day for market share in the desktop and personal computer space. At the same time our customers were doing research on far more dense circuits with no current apparent market, we spent more than five years in R&D developing the products for these customers, for markets that we now call mobile computing—smartphones and tablets. We sacrificed an important portion of our profits for more than five years, including during the global financial crisis years of 2008 and 2009. Some of our competitors did not make these investments. The result? Fast forward to 2013–2015 and the desktop and PC space had become commoditized for electronic chemicals and the mobile computing market boomed. MacDermid enjoyed record revenues and profits. Some of our competitors suffered as the market moved away from them. During the tough years around the financial crisis, we made many short-term moves to cut short-term costs, drive down our purchased costs, and in general squeeze every penny we could *while* continuing to invest in the future.

I had learned earlier about the importance of the golden hour. For someone to deeply think while the phone is ringing or people are walking in and out of the office is unrealistic. Your mind never gets into a deep enough, thoughtful enough state to effectively think about things that have no easy answer. During this period we ran at least a thousand financial models—modeling the impact of "what ifs." What if our growth rate is X or Y, what if we acquired a business for this multiple or that, etc. To process these things in my mind, I would get up very early and write my affirmations, read something philosophical that would get my mind into a receptive state, and then think, think, think. Then four hours later at 9:00 a.m., I would "go to work."

Back to our $100 per share goal: right about the time we established the goal, we ran smack into a recession. Four years later, our share price hadn't moved a nickel. We knew the improvements we had made in the business were important value generators and would show through in spades if we got a little help from the economy, but the recessionary pressures prevented us from proving it. Thinking deeply about our best alternatives, we concluded our best move would be to buy ourselves. We decided to buy back 25 percent of our outstanding shares in a tender offer. Our logic was that our shares would be far more valuable once the economy improved and our improvements could be more clearly seen. We announced the tender offer to buy 25 percent of the outstanding shares that had closed the day before at twenty-four dollars, for thirty dollars.

The day we made the announcement on the stock exchange to our investors, I got a call from the fund manager of our second largest shareholder, Fidelity. He told me he was very pleased; we had made his day. During this time, MacDermid had 3.5 million shares outstanding. By traditional standards, this was a ridiculously small number. Most companies had 10 or even 100 times more shares outstanding. So here was this small company, with far too few shares outstanding, offering to buy back one-fourth of them. The fund manager from Fidelity told me the day we announced the buyback he had been trying to figure out how to get out of his position in Mac-Dermid, as it was too illiquid, or too few shares outstanding. He went on to say, "It's too bad for your other shareholders, as this will be a twenty dollar stock after this deal closes."

We'll get back to that in a moment. First, here is another prime example of thinking deeply: One of my mentors, Tom Smith, had taught me that the number of shares outstanding was a meaningless metric. Here is an example: a company has $100,000 in earnings with 10,000 shares outstanding. That would mean earnings per share of $10 ($100,000/10,000 shares). If the company had a market multiple of twenty times earnings, the share price would be earnings per share of $10 multiplied by twenty or $200 per share. The value of the company would be $2 million (10,000 shares x $200 per share = $2 million).

Let's suppose the company decided to double the shares outstanding. Some think because they are increasing the shares outstanding, they are signaling confidence. However, it is just not true that doubling the shares outstanding means anything at all. If we double the shares outstanding, we now have 20,000 shares instead of 10,000. Good, so far. But we have the same $100,000 in earnings. Now we have to divide the $100,000 by 20,000 instead of 10,000, so the result is $5 per share instead of $10. We multiply the $5 by 20,000 shares outstanding, times the multiple of twenty. What do we get? The same company value of $2 million. Exactly the same place we started. The conclusion? It makes absolutely no difference how many shares are outstanding.

Back to Fidelity. The portfolio manager sold his shares at $30, and he felt great. I hung up the phone a little worried. What if he was right? *No,* I thought deeply. *He can't be right.* Fast-forward a year and the shares were trading for $100, as all the hard work to position MacDermid to take advantage of a turn in the economy came to pass. No one but Tom Smith and I believed. We thought deeply.

Thinking deeply resulted in a pretty nice outcome. When I became CEO in 1990, MacDermid had $8 million in earnings and a market value of $80 million. Without raising a dollar of new equity, and in fact, by reducing our equity by $30 million in the1994 buyback, we ended up in 2013 with $180 million in earnings and $1.8 billion in market value. And it's much higher today.

CHAPTER 7

PRINCIPLE 7:
Create a Culture

*Part of company culture is path-dependent—
it's the lessons you learn along the way.*

—JEFF BEZOS

Culture is the way we act when no one is looking. It is the normal behavior that is unique to our nation, region, family, or in this case, business. Many or perhaps most businesses do not have a distinct culture. That is why you read stories about young people these days being portable, moving from business to business with no emotional connection. That is because there is no glue holding them to a particular company. The most important feature of a successful culture is a feeling of belonging and that someone really cares about you and what you do.

MacDermid was successful beyond anyone's wildest dreams—beginning in 1990, the year I became CEO. In what I refer to as the modern era, starting with less than $10 million in earnings, we transformed the company. When we merged with Platform twenty-three years later, we were earning just short of $200 million. We did that without raising *any* equity capital.

It's in the kilt, mon! And the kilt was somewhat synonymous with our culture.

No image better describes MacDermid's success better than the top 100 managers dressed in their Scottish finest. The kilt had a very long history at MacDermid. Archie MacDermid, the founder and a first-generation Scottish immigrant, had a custom kilt made in Scotland for my father in the 1950s. My father wore it with pride for the better part of forty years. Then in a public ceremony in 1990, when I became CEO, my father presented it to me. That moment is one of the most memorable of my life.

In that one instant, my father validated me. I had gone from a black sheep to the keeper of the culture. I couldn't have been more proud. Our clan bagpiper led me, with tears of pride streaming down my face, in a procession. I paraded past the employees, referred to as the Clan MacDermid, which had gathered for our annual celebration.

"Clan" is the Scottish word for family. The concept of the Scottish clan represented the fighting spirit of MacDermid. We were a small company and were scrappy, like the historic Scottish Highlanders, and this distinction was widely known in the industry. In fact, company plaid jackets were our norm at trade shows for years.

As honored as I was to wear the kilt, I felt it inappropriately placed too much importance on me. Maybe due to my learning disabilities growing up, I never fell into the trap of thinking I was all-important. Yes, I hoped my passion and clear vision could lead us to success, but not without a lot of help. Therefore, I felt uncomfortable placing too much attention on myself. Being the "one" wearing the kilt, as proud as I was, just didn't feel right.

I came up with a solution—we would all wear the kilt! Three months before an offsite meeting, which the top 100 managers would be attending, we got everyone's measurements and had kilts fitted for them. During the afternoon, the staff put kilts in each attendee's room along with instructions to wear the kilt to dinner. Were they ever surprised when they went back to their rooms—and what a sight it was when 100 of them showed up for dinner in a kilt. This was a powerful signal to all of them that it wasn't about me. It was about *us*. What fun we had! We wore those kilts every year at our annual offsite meeting for the rest of my tenure. In fact, one year, we held meetings at Disney Orlando and paraded through Epcot, bringing everything to a halt.

The key wasn't just the symbolism, although I believe it was important. MacDermid was a global enterprise with 2,500 employees. Much, if not all, of our success came from folks who understood their jobs, were driven to succeed, and were given the latitude to do it their way. There are some businesses where a few big decisions can have a big impact on success or failure. Ours wasn't one of those. Our operations were spread over thirty countries in virtually every time zone. Our success depended on real-time decisions at the local level.

One of our real keys to success was the culture that encouraged local managers to make decisions—an unusual strategy/philosophy. We proved over many years that it is effective to rely on empowering the person at the decision point. That is, expecting the employee closest to the particular situation to solve the problem without having to stop and ask for permission. This is the approach that Warren Buffett practices with the managers of Berkshire companies. Sam Walton, founder of Walmart, did it with his store managers, too. But it is not common.

We found it difficult to put this practice in place in acquisitions because the managers of acquired businesses were used to traditional environments and had been told what to do for years. They really struggled with being independent and accountable and depended on a rulebook in many cases. This was the usual dilemma we faced, and we almost always had to move longstanding MacDermid managers into the leadership of acquired companies.

In rulebook-driven strategy, there is limited scope for exercising individual initiative and creativity; it doesn't allow for deep thinking. In rule-based companies, people become political. The unintended consequence of this is a thought process along the lines of "What can I get away with?" At MacDermid, we had few rules. The ones we did have could be considered values, such as *operate with integrity* and *treat people with respect*. Most important, we asked people to exercise good judgment. We didn't dictate what good judgment was. The two ways to learn good judgment are: 1) exercise bad judgment and learn from the experience, and 2) study, learning your craft so you develop mental representations to guide you and thereby learn the easy way by avoiding mistakes to begin with. At MacDermid, we did a lot of both.

We spent time talking about having the "guts to fail." We meant that we wanted folks to make mistakes of commission—i.e., when in doubt, go for it. We believed hesitation and doubt were more destructive than giving it the old entrepreneurial try despite having those feelings. Of course, we didn't want people making attempts that had not been thought through, but we believed that if you wait until you are "sure" of your decision, the opportunity often passes you by.

Most of the examples of failure were relatively small ones. Especially when encountering new problems, simply subjecting the problem to deep thinking isn't enough. Sometimes only trial and error works. As people grew in the organization, they were expected to make larger and larger bets, but they had learned from previous mistakes along the way and used the experience to think deeply, so their success rate was high.

We spent a lot of effort, time, and money teaching the craft. Every employee was offered a four-day seminar on success principles called "Psychology of Achievement." People's lives were changed as they learned many of the impediments and limitations they held were self-imposed. We gave them the tools to break free of these limitations. It was important enough to me that I personally facilitated many of the four-day sessions. We hired experts to teach us about quality systems, sales approaches, strategy, and finance. We put all of our managers through a course called "Owner Earnings," where we spent several days learning about financial modeling and decision-making for value creation. This was an intense early-morning to late-night course that fundamentally changed the way executives viewed decision-making.

One year, each of the top 100 managers received one share of Berkshire Hathaway stock as part of their bonus, and then we took them to the Berkshire annual meeting. I believe it was an amazing learning experience for these people. All of these investments in tools—over time—created a group of leaders who were very unusual in their capabilities and understanding. They used these enhanced mental representations to make better decisions than their competitors or peers, thus generating huge wealth for themselves and our shareholders.

This deep culture made it difficult for the managers of businesses we acquired to fit in. As I mentioned earlier, when we acquired companies, we almost always had to replace management. The MacDermid culture was very difficult for acquired management teams to accept; they just couldn't mesh with our high-performance culture. They were often focused on their fancy company cars, offices, titles, and other perks.

One story I still chuckle about involved one of the CEOs of an acquired company who had two cell phones. When I asked about them, he told me that one was for business on weekdays and the other was for personal use seven days a week. I vividly recall thinking, *This guy will never make it.* He lasted less than a year. It's not that I expected our executives to work all weekend, every weekend, but we ran a global business. We couldn't ask our managers around the world to wait to contact us at headquarters until after the weekend. It was a workday somewhere. So checking in seven days a week to be sure important and timely issues were addressed was expected.

As we were becoming more profitable—fundamentally more profitable—we started with operating margins of 15 percent and ended up at 25 percent. As you've already learned, we knew there was a big opportunity by eliminating duplicate costs in acquired businesses. When you acquire a business, there is generally duplication in administrative or back office operations. Since there would be natural overlaps, my starting point was always the goal of zero duplication. That meant complete elimination of the duplicate costs from the acquired companies. We didn't always make it to the zero goal, but we got awfully close—a strategy virtually no one was following in those days. By dramatically lowering the target acquisition duplicate costs, we increased the starting point profitability, which allowed us to pay back the money we borrowed to acquire the business much more quickly.

In the early days at MacDermid, we knew our costs were too high. As CEO I took an owner mentality and questioned *every* expenditure and inspired my team to do the same. No cost was too small to challenge. For example, I noticed that, since I worked late most evenings, the office cleaning crew wasn't able to clean my office often. I also noticed that my office looked the same as those who had theirs cleaned every day. Okay, I had to take out my own trash and tidy up just a little each day. Ultimately, I asked what we were paying for office cleaning and what it might cost if we had the offices cleaned twice a week instead of every day. Well, we saved $100,000 a year with this change. Some argued, it's only a $100,000, and in the scale of a company with $8 million in profits, it's peanuts, to which I responded, "You wouldn't say that if it was *your* hundred K!"

That is the whole idea of thinking like an owner. There were hundreds of other examples. At budget time I reviewed every line item of every department's budget, worldwide, many thousands of line items. I challenged a few thousand dollars at a time.

You might wonder if this is really the job of the CEO. I would say absolutely not, unless you are teaching people to build a clock. The principle of clock building versus telling time was introduced by James C. Collins and Jerry I. Porras in the bestselling book *Built to Last: Successful Habits of Visionary Companies*. Collins explains that a brilliant manager who goes around telling people what to do every day is not scalable. That is because there is only so much capacity in any one person, no matter how smart and capable he or she is. Collins called that style of operating "the genius and a thousand helpers." On the other hand, teaching, coaching, and leading people can create a sustaining and high-performing enterprise of infinite scale. The old proverb, "Give a man a fish, and you feed him for a day; teach him to fish, and you feed him for a lifetime," is particularly appropriate here. When I showed my colleagues at MacDermid how to think deeply about costs, the next time something like the office cleaning costs came up, I didn't have to get involved.

Sure, cutting costs, even small ones matter, but establishing a cost culture where *everyone* thinks like an owner is far more powerful. I was leading by example. We were also reinforcing a culture of frugality. Many people hated waste just as much as I do, but in the early days, I didn't feel it was embraced as a central cultural principle. It is difficult for one employee to work one way and his neighbor another.

When a culture is strong, people will opt in . . . and out. It is important to establish strong cultural guideposts, and doing so requires looking deeply and thinking deeply about what the culture currently is and where it needs to go. Believe it or not, it is good for people to look in the mirror and say, "This is not for me." You want them to leave so your culture can mesh. It doesn't mean they are not capable; they are just not a fit for the culture.

We weeded out a lot of naysayers in the early years. Most of them left thinking we were crazy. As it turned out, they left many millions of dollars of personal wealth behind so they could go elsewhere and work in an easier environment. I always wished them well. We described the culture as rigorous, not ruthless. By that we meant that we would not compromise our culture, but we would be kind as we ushered out people who didn't fit in.

Perhaps the most important ritual at MacDermid was the annual corporate day. Starting as a small picnic at my father's farm when there were only fifty employees, it grew into an all-day event for hundreds. It began with the "Address to the Clan" in which I presented the "latest." The "latest what" was a little controversial.

We once invited a guy who was applying for a senior management position to corporate day, and he fed back to us his disappointment over the content of the address. He was looking for a traditional state of the company presentation.

What I presented was anything but traditional. I presented theories around how to be successful, similar to the content in this book. My address would be a complete miss with an audience of traditional managers (as it was with this guy); they just don't get the concept that by helping each team (clan) member achieve her or his personal success, the organization would bond together under common ideals, and each successful person, compounding with like-minded others, would carry the organization to overall success. However, for the Clan MacDermid, the speech was a huge success. We gave employees tools to prosper in their personal lives for the good of us all, and we avoided hiring someone who would be a misfit in our culture. Win-win.

We had a lot of fun with the "Address to the Clan" over the years. We often used movies to illustrate the message. We would edit a movie into around three twenty-minute segments, including movies like *Top Gun* (twice), *Braveheart,* and *Apollo 13*. Between each segment, I would illustrate its connection to success principles. One year we had a symphony orchestra perform and talk about the leadership dynamics of an orchestra. One year I dressed up as Freddie Mercury and lip-synched Queen songs to demonstrate being outside one's comfort zone—and, oh man, was I *ever*!

Perhaps the most important part of the corporate day each year was the Clan Bake, a takeoff on clambake, a traditional New England picnic. It was a great gathering highlighted by an award ceremony. This is where I dressed up in the kilt as my father had done before me. Then, in the early days, everyone would receive a service award at five-year increments. Later, as the company grew, we presented five- and ten-year awards locally and fifteen years of service and up at corporate day. I would tell a story about each person, and they would come up to the front of the group with their spouse and often children to receive the award. I took pride in the authenticity of my remarks about each person. People can see right through an embellished story, and besides and most important, you can always find something nice to say about anyone. This sometimes represented the crowning moment of a person's life. There were often many joyful tears all around. Newcomers often told me that it wasn't until this ceremony that they really understood the MacDermid culture.

Much of the glue that held MacDermid together was the MacDermid Philosophy, which was written by the employees in the early 1960s. It was my guiding light, and it withstood the test of time all the way to 2015 when I retired.

Philosophy

Our Business

MacDermid, Incorporated is in the international business of researching, developing, acquiring, manufacturing, marketing, and servicing, for optimum profit to us and our customers, specialty chemicals and systems for the metal and plastic finishing, electronics, graphic arts and offshore oil industries — in accordance with accepted ecologic and social considerations.

Our Customers

We will create an industry image that automatically causes people in the industries we serve to think first of MacDermid.

We will justify their action by first thinking of the customers' needs — what's right for them makes it right for MacDermid by supplying a total system including processes, know-how and services that assist in meeting all their needs.

Our People

We continue to believe in the supreme worth of the individual and the dignity of his or her work for the benefit of all.

We will provide the opportunity for our people to fulfill satisfactorily their own personal objectives and ambitions and reward them in proportion to their contribution toward achieving the Corporate objectives.

We will continue to be a place of opportunity where people "have the guts to fail." We will encourage the entrepreneurs and innovators. We will continually challenge the goals, objectives, organization and all the operating and procedural aspects of our business and modify them when needed.

Our progress and your progress, our Company's long-term advantage and your long-term advantage, lie in our human resources. Other advantages that come about from technological improvements, the opening of new markets, lower costs, etc., all prove to be relatively short run. So, basically, it is the initiative, the will and the motivation that people bring to their work on which we rely for our survival and growth.

We will continue to try to attract new people who have creative and probing minds; people who will at times be disturbing—questioning policy and procedures. If we are wise, we will welcome it, resolve it, put it to work, or forget it.

We will continue to expand with the best possible talent available and continue to train them, and ourselves, so that we each increase our ability to contribute to the Company's progress.

We will each strive to exemplify the MacDermid Spirit of teamwork and cooperation throughout the organization, which has been instrumental to our past and present growth as a corporation.

What We Expect From You

First and foremost, we expect of you a fundamental honesty—honesty with yourself, with your Company and with all those with whom you interact, whether they be associates within our organization, our customers or society in general. Character and strength have always been born of honesty and a willingness to face up to the truth of each situation as it arises.

Second, we expect and insist on hard work. An easy life, marked by the absence of difficulty, builds neither character nor happiness. We believe that self-realization of the individual is founded on accomplishment, which implies a willingness to make the sacrifices necessary to get the job done the way it should be done.

Third, we expect you to accept responsibility. Every assignment you will have carries with it a responsibility for accomplishment. Commit yourself to achievement which you consider beyond the scope of your talents and then program your effort to translate it into a reality.

Fourth, we expect of you a loyalty—loyalty to yourself, your family, your associates, your organization and our customers. We have always worked together as an organization and your own personal achievements will be measured in terms of the contribution you make to our joint effort.

Fifth, we expect you to demonstrate good judgment. Judgment is essentially an ability to appraise facts. Factual knowledge must come before good judgment. This means you must continually educate yourself on our Company, our products and our industry. In this way, you will have the material on which a sound appraisal of good judgment is based.

This is what we expect of you, and being in an extremely competitive environment, we have a real urgency in this expectancy.

What You Can Expect From Us

One, you can expect from us the fairest treatment of which we are capable—fair in respect to matters of compensation, fair in respect to working conditions and fair in respect to personnel policies.

Two, you can expect from us, as a Company, complete honesty in whatever we do. Your assignments will never compromise the principles of honesty and common decency which we also expect you, as an individual, to uphold.

Three, you can expect that we will provide assignments which will represent challenges to you—assignments which will enable you to grow toward your professional and personal objectives.

Four, you can expect that we will offer opportunities for advancement. Our desire is to grow from within.

Five, you can expect that we will be a demanding organization—demanding of your time, your talents and the best which you as an individual have to offer. In this way our company will grow and you will grow with it.

I am an Objectivist, an adherent of Objectivism, which is a philosophical system developed by Ayn Rand, author of *Atlas Shrugged* and other notable books. Objectivists follow Rand's philosophy of reason, individualism, and capitalism. She philosophizes that the person is the center of the universe. If each person organizes and takes responsibility for her life, then combined as a society, we will all prosper. She advocated for reason and reality for what it is. She was against altruism in favor of benevolence, preferring that one choose to be generous, not made to feel guilty to do so.

I believe the original employees who penned the Mac-Dermid philosophy must have been influenced by Rand. The convergence between the principles of Objectivism and the MacDermid philosophy is remarkable. At MacDermid, we believed in the power of the individual, as the MacDermid philosophy says, "We continue to believe in the supreme worth of the individual and the dignity of his or her work for the benefit of all." It goes on to say, "It is the initiative, the will and the motivation that people bring to their work on which we rely for our survival and growth." You see, there is nothing in The Formula that depends on anyone other than yourself. I believe you make your own luck, you attract the right colleagues, and the circumstances that lead to success will open to you as you follow this path.

That is not to say the culture was focused all on the individual. We believed in teamwork, as the philosophy says, "We will each strive to exemplify the MacDermid spirit of teamwork and cooperation throughout the organization, which has been instrumental to our past and present growth as a corporation." In fact, the whole concept of clan is built around teamwork. We worked closely together. We supported each other. But we didn't wait around when we saw a dropped ball by asking whose ball it was; we picked it up. Our culture was built around individual initiative for the benefit of us all.

The examples of the philosophy in action are many. There were multiple times someone way down in the organization pushed back about a policy, pointing out it was inconsistent with the philosophy. How many times did we celebrate failure? So many I can't keep count. It was virtually impossible to get fired for trying and failing. Not trying was a much bigger problem. For that you could get in trouble.

I spent a huge amount of my personal time reinforcing the philosophy. By the time someone had been at MacDermid five years, they would have been fully indoctrinated. It wasn't for everyone though. Just like Apple or Walmart, traditional "professional managers" need not apply.

The philosophy was evident in our compensation practices. We paid modest base salaries, but offered generous performance bonuses. Our total bonus pool often reached millions of dollars, which accomplished two things: The bonus pool shared the success in good years, and it softened the downside in not-so-good years. We also offered stock programs very deep in the organization. Most companies offer stock options to the top twenty managers; we offered options to the top 200.

My favorite story is when one of our truck drivers came into my office and presented me with a bottle of champagne. When I asked what it represented, he said, "I just wanted to say thank you, as my profit-sharing plan balance just topped one million dollars." This man had never made over forty thousand dollars. Yee-haw!

There were many millionaires at MacDermid. How we constructed our stock ownership plans was unusual and very important. I do not believe in normal stock option plans where you get a fixed right to buy shares at some modest amount over the current stock price in the future. The proponents of such a plan argue that if the stock price goes up in the future, everyone wins, so why not share that with the management that helps create the higher stock price?

The problem with this rationale is complex, but essentially there are two fundamental problems: 1) Management gets to keep and reinvest the earnings of the business, so that even an incompetent manager should easily be able to make the stock price go up by reinvesting retained earnings. Even putting money in a savings account will cause the balance to grow; and 2) Skin in the game. Stock options offer only upside, as there is no investment required by the recipient. This incents management to take risks because there is only upside. When we were negotiating our go-private transaction in 2007, the private equity firm's lawyer called me and said, "There must be a mistake in your roll-over investment as your ownership stake is the same as your MacDermid holdings before the transaction."

There was no mistake. I explained that I was rolling over 100 percent of my holdings in the public MacDermid to invest in the new private MacDermid. The lawyer told me she had never seen that done. No risk, no reward. I was so convinced we would be successful that I wanted to maximize my owner-ship stake in the new private MacDermid. The result? When the company was sold in 2013, my investment, along with the investors who I brought in to the deal, profited by three times our 2007 investment. For every dollar we invested, we received three in return when the company was sold.

As we conclude this discussion of the final principle of The Formula and move on to Part Two, we transition to a series of chapters on my heroes. In each case, I discuss the principles of The Formula as they relate to uber-successful individuals, some famous, some not. Just as we used the science behind The Formula to show its efficacy beyond my experiences, these individuals are outstanding examples of The Formula at work. All of my heroes had modest starts and ended up huge successes. None of them followed a traditional path.

PART TWO

The Formula
in Action:
Meet the Heroes

CHAPTER 8

Tom Smith

Consult your friend on all things, especially on those which respect yourself. His counsel may then be useful where your own self-love might impair your judgment.

—LUCIUS ANNAEUS SENECA

In addition to my duties as an analyst at MacDermid, one of my first assignments was investor relations, which entailed keeping our shareholders informed. Coordinating communication and scheduling between our CEO and vital shareholders and analyzing changes in share ownership by our major holders gave me the opportunity to sit in meetings between our CEO and other senior managers with our large shareholders. Our biggest shareholder by far was Tom Smith, my second and greatest mentor.

Tom is one of the most insightful investors ever to live. If you invested $10,000 with Tom at the inception of his investment firm in 1974, the investment would be worth $4 million today. Along the way, you would have doubled your money every 4.2 years, decade after decade. The catch is, you couldn't readily invest with Tom as his fund had been closed to new investors for most of those years. He was closed to new investors because he was so successful, he didn't need any more money to invest. He propelled his company, Prescott Investors, from assets of a few million dollars in 1974 to billions today, with hundreds of millions in negative paid-in-capital, meaning his investors have taken out many multiples of what they put in. Under Tom's leadership, Prescott has enjoyed Berkshire Hathaway–like results, with compound returns hitting the high teens for more than forty years. I think of Tom as "The Unknown Buffett." And unlike Warren Buffett, who was unlikely to mentor me, Tom did.

There is no way around it: a mentor is one of the cornerstones of success and should probably be the eighth unofficial principle of The Formula. Mentoring activates and accelerates the components of The Formula. In Tom, I recognized someone who could teach me how to build and run a world-class business. When I first met Tom, it was my job to facilitate answering his questions during his visits to our offices. My rapport with him built quickly to the point where I was asking him more questions than he was asking us.

I was taken by Tom's unique approach. Other investors who visited asked about short-term results and pestered us to give them insight to the next quarter's profits. Tom was all about the long term and encouraged us to think about growing longer term even at the expense of the immediate results. When he would leave to go to his car, I'd literally follow him out to the parking lot, peppering him with questions the whole way, until he'd have to close the car door and roll up his window to get rid of me. Even at that point, Tom never seemed to mind me hounding him or my hunger to learn. He was patient and generous. Over time, he explained his investing philosophy—taking big stakes in a small set of companies and holding investments for years, not months. He explained what habits and traits made certain business leaders not just great, but dependably and consistently great. He introduced me to the wisdom and stories of Warren Buffett and Sam Walton, among others.

What was in it for Tom? Tom was twenty years my elder with vastly more experience, so it wasn't realistic he was going to learn from me. Why would he devote his time and energy to coaching me? I can't assume his reasons, but I have come to learn that great mentors give of themselves for the sheer joy of seeing their protégés succeed, especially the ones who show the characteristics of being able to become world class in their own right. A mentor's satisfaction comes from seeing the effect of his or her wisdom invested in another. Often a mentor's motivation comes from simply giving back. Tom had not taken his success for granted. In fact, like many other success stories, he started very modestly.

Raised by a single mom, Tom attended college on the GI Bill. He told me once that he realized his success was based on several factors: smart, hard work, yes, but also a measure of good fortune. As such, he felt that giving back was the right thing to do. And what better way than to multiply your wisdom through others?

You can, of course, repay mentors simply by saying thank you, acknowledging their gift, and letting them know you are grateful. You can tell them how much you appreciate their time. You also can show them your eagerness to receive more instruction by using verbal cues such as "That sounds interesting" or "I'd like to hear more about that, please." It really helps to keep your mouth shut and be a good listener.

The recipient of mentoring, after all, has to be willing to confess how much he or she doesn't know. One has to be willing to submit to the instruction of a master and be willing to be vulnerable in order to receive. Not everyone views these acts as strengths. Many view them as signs of weakness, and thus are unwilling to enter into the process and relationship.

How do you find a mentor? If you have humility and are willing to leave your ego at the door, you won't have to look. Potential mentors will sense your receptivity and will find you.

Below are twenty years of Tom's lessons. The lessons will seem strange. They surely are not common wisdom. You don't turn thousands into millions by following the herd. Tom's genius is being able to cast his eyes over a sea of companies and pick out the few that had the potential to grow their share price tenfold or more. Much of Wall Street "wisdom" is largely the opposite of the way Tom thinks and acts. He is a concentrated investor, making a small number of huge relative bets in the most unlikely companies. Wall Street would largely avoid the companies Tom invested in. They would view them as too small and therefore too risky. They would do minimal deep research and therefore get put off by the industry headlines, heuristic shortcuts, and research biases. The adage "Put your eggs in a basket and watch that basket" speaks to how he thinks. Unlike the typical Wall Street investor, he pays little attention to what the market does every day. This investor with a fund of more than a billion dollars doesn't have a stock quote machine on his desk. I learned many things from Tom, enough for a whole book, but here are the top-ten lessons I learned from him, with #1 being the most important.

10. Taxes matter.

9. Market downturns are your friend.

8. Buy stocks as if you were buying the entire company.

7. Management is paramount.

6. The moat, or sustainable competitive advantage, is a major determinant of value.

5. Capital allocation is key.

4. Patience is a virtue.

3. Buy companies, not markets.

2. It's all about free cash flow . . . per share.

1. Remember the power of compounding.

Taxes Matter

Tom believes deeply in the power of compounding of free cash flow. Taxes come before "free cash flow." How a company manages their taxes is important because any savings in taxes is a direct credit to cash flow. Taxes affect the investor in other ways, too. Short-term gains double your taxes compared to long-term capital gains. Holding good companies for long periods allows you to compound pretax as no tax is due until you sell. Tom often holds good companies for many years, allowing pretax compounding to work for him.

Market Downturns Are Your Friend

Tom spends a lot of time educating management teams about the power of buying back stock. By doing so he explains how one concentrates ownership by giving each remaining share a greater portion of the future. Downturns also provide entry points to invest in good companies. Tom sometimes follows companies for years, but doesn't buy them because they are too expensive. But, occasionally, something happens. Maybe there is a liability that the market is worried about or a regulatory issue or a product introduction failure or just an overall market panic that has nothing to do with the target company. Sometimes these issues cause the stock of the affected company to go way down. The key is to understand whether the issue is fundamental to the company's future or if it is more noise because you can be sure the "herd mentality" of Mr. Market is to sell, sell, sell. That's when Tom buys, buys, buys.

Buy Stocks as if You Were Buying the Entire Company

The mindset difference between buying a share of stock and buying an entire company can be huge. Think about it: If you are buying an entire company, you are betting large sums on an illiquid asset. You just can't change your mind and sell it a little later. It generally is a big risk to buy an entire company. Tom would argue buying a share of stock should be no different. Just because the investment is more modest and it is more liquid doesn't mean you should be any less diligent about your investigation of the company. Warren Buffett calls it the "punch card concept," where you think of each investment as if you were granted a punch card. The catch is you only get five punches in your entire lifetime. Think of the care you would exhibit if you only had five punches in your lifetime. That is precisely how you should treat every investment.

Management Is Paramount

Tom spends a large amount of time with management of the companies he is considering investing in. It is hard to judge critical leadership traits like honesty and integrity. However, without those traits, would you buy the entire company? If you did not trust management enough to be your partner, why would you buy a share of stock in his company? And honesty and integrity are just the beginning of the traits it takes to be a good leader. Judgment is also key. The principles in this book require thought—that is, "think deeply." Part of

Tom's magic is educating leaders. Some, like me, certainly have the capacity to learn but perhaps not the experience. This is where Tom really shines. He takes the time to meet with management and introduce them to these principles, such that one day they own them.

The Moat, or Sustainable Competitive Advantage, Is a Major Determinant of Value

Really good businesses have a moat or a source of competitive advantage. Think of a moat—a water-filled ditch—surrounding a medieval castle. It was designed to protect the inhabitants of the castle from attackers. There was a draw bridge, which could be lifted at times of impending attack, and allow the castle to be protected by the moat, preventing attackers from accessing the castle. In the business context, a moat is a characteristic of a business that protects it from competitors. Typically that is in the form of maintaining a company's competitive advantage. Examples of moats include barriers established by years and years of advertising. If a competitor wants to break into a well-established consumer market, it can take years and many millions of dollars to generate consumer awareness that an established brand already enjoys.

Think of ketchup. Of course the name that comes to mind is Heinz. Good luck trying to break into that market. Sometimes competitive advantage can result from investment. The classic example is jet engines. It costs billions to develop a new engine. Given the revenue that existing players, in this case GE, Pratt & Whitney, and Rolls-Royce have to fund new engine development, it is highly unlikely a new competitor can enter this market.

Technology protected by a patent is one of the widest moats. While a patent is in force, competitors are legally prevented from entering the market. This patent moat, or competitive advantage, is common in the pharmaceutical industry. One of the best examples of a moat caused by a patent is Pfizer Incorporated's anti-cholesterol medication, Lipitor, the best-selling medication of all time. Patented in 1999, the drug entered the market after all approvals in 1996. Lipitor generated revenues of $125 billion for Pfizer from 1996 to 2012. During the 14.5 years Lipitor was patent-protected, no one else was able to sell the product.

MacDermid had a moat, in the form of the competitive advantage of employing most of the technical experts in the technologies it produced and sold. There are only so many experts in these technologies, and virtually all of them work for MacDermid or its top couple of competitors. The moat is derived from having so many of these people, which makes it difficult for a new entrant to enter their markets. What's a new entry to do? Place an advertisement for a thousand technical specialists?

The other example of MacDermid's moat is the very complex chemistry of its products. The complex formulations are difficult to copy. The combination of these two factors results in high relative margins for products, even though they are not protected by patents. When calculating MacDermid's intrinsic value, one can be more confident in the margin profile's sustainability over time. Nevertheless, once you have a moat, it is critical you maintain it. Staying awake at night thinking others are trying to figure out how to eat your lunch is not all bad, because worthy opponents are surely out to get you.

Moats don't always last forever. For example, if a moat is derived from a patent, the moat ends as soon as the patent expires. That is called a patent cliff. Using the patent example, if in your intrinsic value model, you included an assumption of steady growth, in perpetuity, you would be far off. That is because as soon as the patent expired, new entries would come into the market, thereby reducing your revenues and profits. On the date the patent expires, competitors are allowed to copy the product. Lipitor again is a good example. Lipitor generated about $15 billion in revenues the last year of its patent. It sold Lipitor for an average cost to the patient of $160 per month. Soon after the patent expired in 2011 and generic copies were introduced, the cost to the patient of the generics was reduced to $10 per month. Sales of the branded Lipitor dropped from $15 billion to $3 billion, as the moat evaporated.

Sustaining competitive advantage is another reason you need to be passionate about your business. To stay ahead of the competition, you have to excel in innovation, keeping one step ahead of the competition and never resting on your laurels, especially the patent laurels. If you avoid costs that are unnecessary, you will have more to invest in innovation and other areas of differentiation. Then, and only then, will you have a chance of staying ahead. In the end, competitive advantage is not stagnant. At MacDermid, we enjoyed margins far above industry averages—for seventy-five years! It was only possible by innovating and reinventing ourselves with passion and determination.

Engine manufacturers only maintain their moat if they continue to invest in new engines. Consumer product manufacturers dissipate their moat if they stop advertising. Pharmaceutical manufacturers know their moats will end when their patents do, so continuing to invest in R&D to come up with new drugs or acquiring smaller innovators is critical to their long-term health.

Capital Allocation Is Key

Most managers do not think a lot about capital allocation. Generally they retain the cash flow generated in the business. Sometimes they pay dividends. Almost all treat capital expenditures as sunk costs necessary to run the business. This is a very misguided way to think about business. If cash flow is what determines value, every dollar of capital in a business is extremely valuable. There are always multiple competing interests for that capital. They all have a cost and a return profile. Capital expenditures for plant and equipment that lead to high-quality growth and returns on investment, far above the firm's cost of capital, can be very worthwhile investments. Often the key in the decision process is the assumptions used in the models to calculate returns. Quite often, assumptions are too optimistic. Those who propose the capital project often project too high of revenues or too much enhanced productivity as a result of the investment. A high-quality manager pushes back on these assumptions and forces them to be realistic. My belief is when in doubt, just say no.

Acquisitions fall into the same category. A tremendous amount of shareholder wealth has been frittered away with poor acquisitions. Capital can be used for dividends, returning capital to shareholders. However, dividends can be less tax effective as corporate earnings have already been taxed once and dividends are taxed again. Additionally, with dividends, the market comes to expect them and it is difficult to reduce them, even if in the following periods far higher returns can be made elsewhere. That leaves share buybacks as a use of capital, one of Tom's favorites. By reducing the shares over time, the remaining shares permanently own a higher percentage of the company's future. This can be a powerful, tax-effective compounder of the increase in shareholder value per share.

Patience Is a Virtue

Clearly business is a marathon not a sprint. Enduring businesses are not built overnight. In describing investing, Warren Buffett talks about waiting for the fat pitch, a baseball analogy. Here is what he says: "The stock market is a no-called-strike game. You don't have to swing at everything—you can wait for your perfect pitch. The problem when you're a money manager is, your fans keep yelling, 'Swing, you bum!'"[16] Tom is famous for following companies for years, waiting for them to "go on sale." Tom has no bias for action, spending his time thinking deeply, waiting for the right opportunity. By the time I became CEO of MacDermid, Tom had owned the stock for the better part of fifteen years. It had been a nice returning, if not spectacular, investment until we worked together to take it to the next level. Then, in a few short years, he made another ten times on his investment.

Buy Companies Not Markets

Like I said, Tom has no quote machine on his desk. No trading department. This is because he thinks only about buying great companies at a good value for the long term. Paying a few pennies more or less just doesn't matter for a long-term investor. As we have discussed, the market is not efficient—even though virtually every business school in the country covers the efficient market hypothesis (EMH) in its curriculum. Here is a real-life proof source: In 1994 MacDermid bought back 25 percent of the outstanding shares for thirty

---

16 Buffett, Mary, and David Clark. *The Tao of Warren Buffett: Warren Buffett's Words of Wisdom: Quotations and Interpretations to Help Guide You to Billionaire Wealth and Enlightened Business Management.* New York, NY: Scribner, 2006.

dollars a share when Mr. Market had just the day before put a price of $24 a share. We closed the tender offer, bought the shares, and then within a year, the stock went to $100 per share. Virtually nothing about our story had changed, so which price was right: twenty-four or one hundred? In one case, I would argue the market was depressed, in the other euphoric. It is worth noting that we paid about $30 million for 25 percent of the company we bought back. When we merged with Platform in 2013, the company was valued at $1.8 billion. Twenty-five percent of that? $450 million.

It's All About Free Cash Flow . . . Per Share

Tom is hyper-focused on free cash flow. Few management teams give more than lip service to free cash flow. Most don't even know how to calculate it. Mr. Market has conditioned us to think about earnings per share (EPS), or worse, earnings before interest depreciation and amortization (EBITDA) that is used as a shortcut definition of "profits." It is supposed to equalize for the amount of debt a company has, thereby making companies more comparable. It does equalize for debt, but it completely ignores the need for capital to run a business. With EPS, the problem is the shareholders can't monetize EPS because, as we discussed, earnings are very different from cash, and shareholders can only monetize cash. It is possible to have very high EPS and no cash at all. EBITDA is even worse, as it completely neglects the capital necessary to run the business, interest on borrowings, and taxes. Many companies have failed while having positive EPS or EBITDA. Ultimately, the value of a business has to be the present value of the cash that can be extracted by its owners over the life of the business. As focused as Tom is on cash flow, he is obsessed with measuring it per share.

I wrote a piece in MacDermid's annual report years ago. At the time, our share price was about twenty dollars. There were 30 million shares outstanding, for a value of $600 million. At the time our free cash flow was $100 million. I made the following argument: "Suppose if our share price is unchanged, we buy back $100 million in stock a year. At the end of six years, there would be one share outstanding. Do you think it would still be worth twenty dollars?" This, in spades, demonstrates the power of thinking in per-share terms. Ultimately, we bought the whole company, and the rest is history.

Remember the Power of Compounding

Compounding is generated by the sum of return, multiplied by time. Put another way, compounding means that you earn returns on your returns, thereby multiplying the earnings effect. Take a simple example. Say you have a $1,000 investment that earns 10 percent. Your balance at the end of the first year is $1,100. At the end of the first year and every year thereafter, you can take out the $100 gain and spend it. After twenty years of doing this, you would have your $1,000, plus you would have consumed another $2,000, which is your $100 times twenty years. The total amount over twenty years would be $3,000. But, instead of consuming the $100 every year, suppose you reinvest the gain? At the same 10 percent gain, the following year you would make $110 rather than the $100 you would make if you consumed the prior year's gain. Not that big a deal? Here's where compounding comes in. What if you reinvested your gains every year for the full twenty years? Your balance at the end of twenty years would be $6,727, more than double the $3,000 you would have if you did not take advantage of the power of compounding.

Most people focus on the return side of the formula and forget the time side. But even a small amount compounded over a long time makes a huge difference. That is one of the reasons why success in business is a marathon not a sprint. I was once asked if I would sell MacDermid at double the current stock price. The market value at the time was about $100 million. I responded that $200 million was far too low a price. Common wisdom would say that turning down double your current stock price is crazy, maybe even irresponsible. Ultimately, the value of MacDermid was almost ten times higher than the double that was suggested. I think very few executives would turn down double the market price, but we knew, at the rate we were compounding earnings, it wouldn't be long before we had a far higher stock price.

Think about the $10,000 invested with Tom in 1974. If compounded returns were higher by only 1 percent above what would otherwise be the case (if he wasn't obsessed with after-tax compounding), it would result in a 50 percent higher total return on your original investment all these years later.

How many investors invest almost exclusively in very small companies and then concentrate their investments in a handful of these companies? No diversification by Wall Street standards. Tom's entire strategy is based on thinking deeply. I will never forget the time when I proudly told Tom about our $100 a share goal (when our shares were in the low twenties and had been for three years). Everyone I told laughed at me. Tom? He looked me straight in the eye and said unflinchingly, "Of course you mean after the split?" That means he was suggesting essentially doubling my goal!

Passion? I can't count the number of days Tom said, "This is the greatest day of my life!" I have never met anyone more positive and enthusiastic. I recently attended Tom's ninetieth birthday party. He was as inquisitive and focused as ever.

CHAPTER 9

Sam Walton

*I don't know what causes a person to be ambitious,
but it is a fact that I have been over-blessed
with drive and ambition from the time I hit the
ground. So I have always pursued everything I was
interested in with true passion—some would say
obsession—to win. I always held the bar pretty high
for myself: I've set extremely high personal goals.*

—SAM WALTON

When Sam Walton passed away in 1992, he was the richest man in America, with a net worth of $28 billion. Mr. Walton and his book *Sam Walton: Made in America* had a huge influence on me in my early years as CEO. Many of his principles illustrate the core of The Formula.

Before true discount stores were established around 1950, there was a store category called variety, or five-and-dime stores, signifying a store that sold lots of different merchandise relatively inexpensively, mostly for five and ten cents. The originator of the variety-store concept was the now-defunct chain Woolworth's. Keep in mind that inflation resulted in a huge reduction in dollar-purchasing power. Five cents around 1910 would buy what a dollar does today. Similar stores exist

117

today, but they are called dollar stores. Dollar General and Family Dollar are the most well known. Another variety store was Kresge, which morphed into Kmart.

Walton started by buying one franchised five-and-dime store, called Ben Franklin. The most famous franchise system is McDonald's. The individual McDonald's stores are owned by independent companies that use the name and are supplied by the umbrella organization called a franchisor. In Walton's case, he used the Ben Franklin name and bought merchandise from the umbrella organization. He was the consummate merchant, but what he became best known for was complex distribution. Walton was obsessed with taking the cost out of delivering products to the retail sites.

Success is a marathon, not a sprint, and Sam was not an overnight success. Let's look at Sam Walton's timeline.

- 1945—age 27, acquires first Ben Franklin franchise.

- 1950—age 32, lost lease. Store closed. Opens new Ben Franklin franchise.

- 1960—age 42, 15 stores, $1.9 million in revenue.

- 1962—age 44, opens first Walmart.

- 1967—age 49, Walmart has 19 stores.

- 1970—age 52, Walmart initial public offering (IPO). Walmart has grown to 32 stores. Revenue $31 million.

- 1978—age 60, Walmart has 195 stores, revenue $678 million.

- 1984—age 66, Walmart has 600 stores, revenue $4.5 billion.

- 1991—age 73, Walmart has 3,500 stores, revenue $32 billion. Passes Sears as America's largest retailer.

Sam started his business career with a short stint at JC Penney, followed by military service in World War II. After leaving the service in 1945 at age twenty-seven, he bought a very small, failing Ben Franklin variety-store franchise in Newport, Arkansas. The store had revenues of $72,000 a year. Five years later, he had his first business failure when his landlord would not renew his lease, and he was forced to sell his store. The problem was, there was not a suitable alternative location in that town, so Sam had to move his family and start all over in an entirely new town. And start over he did, with another Ben Franklin franchise in Benton-ville, Arkansas. He spent the next ten years building a small regional chain of variety stores. Bentonville would go on to become famous as the world headquarters of the largest retailer in the world.

By 1960, fifteen years after he started, he was up to fifteen stores doing $1.9 million in revenues, pretty small potatoes—not a track most people would think would lead someone to found the largest retailer in the world. After seventeen years developing his retailing skills, he opened the first Walmart. Sam started Walmart because he had gone to his Ben Franklin franchisors and asked them to reduce the amount of profit margin they charged on merchandise purchased through them. In one of the colossal misjudgments in business history, they refused. Five years later, Walmart was up to nineteen stores. Kmart had two hundred and fifty. Would anyone have given Sam a chance of Walmart surpassing Kmart when the store count was two hundred and fifty to nineteen?

Walmart went public in 1970 with $31 million in revenue. Sam was fifty-two years old. By 1984 Walmart then was up to six hundred stores doing $4.5 billion, and in 1991 Walmart passed Kmart and Sears as the largest retailer in the world with over $32 billion in revenue. Sam was seventy-two years old and had been in business forty-six years. So much for overnight success.

Yes, success is a marathon not a sprint. Realize though, that at the same time, as Walton shows, it is certainly not a stroll in the park. Here is what he had to say about pace and passion:

If I had to single out one element in my life that has made a difference for me, it would be passion to compete. That passion has pretty much kept me on the go, looking ahead to the next store visit, or the next store opening, or the next merchandising item I personally wanted to promote out in the stores. It is a story about entrepreneurship, and risk, and hard work, knowing where you are going and to be willing to do what it takes to get you there. It's a story about believing in your idea even when maybe other folks don't, and about sticking to your guns. But I think more than anything it proves there's absolutely no limit to what plain ordinary working people can accomplish if they are given the opportunity and the encouragement and the incentive to do their best. Because that's how Walmart became Walmart: ordinary people joined together to do extraordinary things. At first we amazed ourselves. And before too long we amazed everybody else.[17]

Walton illustrates that it is not always the people with fancy degrees from prestigious institutions who achieve greatness. In fact, it often is not. Often the people who come from the prestigious backgrounds won't risk failing as they have had so much success growing up, and they don't want

---

17 Walton, Sam, and John Huey. *Sam Walton: Made in America.* New York, NY: Doubleday, 1992.

to risk failure. No one would ever have accused Sam Walton of being fancy or pretentious.

Sam was versatile. He did not just stay in Bentonville, Arkansas, with his head down running his business. When it started to become evident that discount stores were making traction in some parts of the country, Sam traveled all around the United States to visit the stores and the owners to learn about the new trend.

Walton was driven. Walmart had Saturday morning meetings that all management attended. Sam would arrive in the middle of the night to get a jump-start on reading the weekly reports from the stores. By the time everyone else arrived, Sam knew more about the results than the managers responsible for the individual stores.

Walton felt he needed a better way to scout for store locations. So he learned to fly and bought an airplane. Sam exemplified the entrepreneurial spirit of doing whatever it took.

Sam Walton created a unique culture at Walmart. He built the business by hiring the most unlikely managers, small town locals without an advanced education. He promoted very young and inexperienced folks and gave them a chance. Here is what his number-two executive said about Walton's hiring practice:

In my opinion, most of them weren't anywhere near ready to run stores, but Sam proved me wrong. If you take someone who lacks the experience and the know-how but has the real desire to get the job done, he'll make up for what he lacks. And that proved true nine times out of ten. It was one way we were able to grow so fast.[18]

---

18 Walton, Sam, and John Huey. *Sam Walton: Made in America.* New York, NY: Doubleday, 1992.

I believe there is a real winning strategy behind hiring and promoting young people. That was a strategy we followed at MacDermid with great success. Young people tend to be more moldable, willing to try new ideas. That is not to say that older people can't change. They can and do. It's just easier to get younger people to accept new ideas.

Sam on Thinking Deeply

Sam was very focused on the key drivers of his success. It is said he obsessed with the formula for winning in a grand scale unlike anyone in retailing before or since.

I believe it is important to understand the concept of the strategic driver of a business. What I mean by strategic driver is that a single activity, if executed well, will lead to a winning hand, almost regardless of what else is going on. This means the choice of activity is all-important. For some businesses, it might be engineering: how to design factories to be efficient. For others it might be research and development. For Walmart, it was cost and efficiency: getting merchandise to the customers at the lowest cost possible.

Of course, other things mattered. It mattered if the engineering systems in the stores and warehouses worked properly. It mattered if the financial affairs of the company were in order. But all of those things could be average, and if the low-cost merchandising and distribution were executed in an exemplary fashion, Walmart would win. For any business, it is therefore critical that you identify what one thing, executed very well, will cause you to win. This takes deep thought. Sam studied every aspect of the distribution model from buying to warehousing and shipping to merchandising. He was obsessed with low-cost merchandising. There are stories in the early days where he drove his station wagon across the state to load it up with closeout merchandise he had found.

There is a famous story about Sam engaging with the CEO of Procter & Gamble. P&G is one of the largest suppliers of consumer-branded products in the world. Sam told the CEO it was important he come to Bentonville, Arkansas, to meet with him. When the CEO arrived in Bentonville, Sam told him he believed P&G's sales to Walmart equaled P&G's sales to the country of Japan, and he demanded attention at a level of a country. There is now a P&G employee stationed in Bentonville to coordinate with Walmart: the same as if they were an entirely different country.

Walton understood very early on that getting merchandise to the stores efficiently was critical. They spent enormous amounts of money on computer systems, distribution centers, and purchased their own trucking fleets. They were able to take cost out of the entire supply chain and pass the savings along to the consumer.

The fundamental tenet in discounting is about volume. Pricing of consumer general merchandise is highly elastic, meaning that the lower the price, the more volume is sold. The calculation Walton followed was that if they took half the profit per item, they could generate three times the sales volume. This was powerful because that formula resulted in 50 percent more total dollars of profit per category (0.5 x 3 = 1.5).

There were real structural impediments to Walton's emerging discount strategy. The first impediment was the so-called fair trade laws that allowed manufacturers to set retail prices for merchandise. These state laws started cropping up in the 1930s and were very prevalent in the first fifteen years of Sam's career. This had the effect of limiting the brands that discounters could sell. By the mid-seventies these laws were largely repealed, opening up the discount strategy to almost all general consumer-merchandise categories.

The second impediment was Ben Franklin, Walton's franchisor. The franchise agreement required Walton to sell products purchased from Ben Franklin, representing 80 percent of his revenues. To make matters worse, Ben Franklin took a 25 percent cut on the merchandise, dramatically reducing Walton's margins, and restricting his ability to offer discounts. Ultimately, this is what led to the establishment of Walmart. Imagine how the world of discount mega stores would have developed differently if Ben Franklin had met Sam Walton halfway. This was arguably the best thing that ever happened to Walton, as it forced him to strike out on his own and found Walmart.

CHAPTER 10

Warren Buffett

You only have to do a very few things right in your life so long as you don't do too many things wrong.

—WARREN BUFFETT

Warren Buffett is an absolutely legendary investor. Having bought his first stock at age eleven, now at eighty-seven, he has one of the longest track records in the investing business. He started early, focused intensely, and evolved into one of the great minds in business. Interestingly, Buffett's original premise for investing in Berkshire Hathaway was flawed. In his early days as an investor, he followed his college professor Benjamin Graham, another legendary investor, author of *The Intelligent Investor*. Graham believed in buying businesses as cheaply as possible based on asset value. Buffett saw opportunity in Berkshire, an old-line New England textile manufacturer. Its shares were selling for less than the cash the company held. In essence Buffett was getting all the buildings, plant, and equipment for less than zero. Amazing buy, right? Wrong.

As it turned out, the textile business was doomed by low-price competition, first from the Southern United States, then from overseas. As it turned out, the hard assets were worth much less than zero. There was a cost to exit the textile business. Such is the flaw (logical fallacy) in buying businesses based on buying assets cheaply as the single criteria. Buffett's investment thesis was flawed. Nevertheless, under Buffett, Berkshire increased its share price from the $14 per share when he bought his shares to $250,000 per share today. How, you ask, does that fact reconcile with my statement that his thesis in buying Berkshire was flawed? Well, actually, it was only partly flawed. Capital allocation is a very important skill of a great business leader. In buying Berkshire, Buffett got control of all their cash. By brilliantly allocating it, the rest becomes history. So that part of the investment thesis was correct. This shows that you do not have to be 100 percent right to win. There have been many books written about Buffett. I recommend you read anything you come across about him. Here we will take the parts of the Buffett philosophy that were the most instrumental in developing The Formula.

Thinking Deeply—Weighing versus Voting

Buffett believes most deeply in the concept of intrinsic value defined as the total amount of cash that can be taken out of the business by its owners over the life of the business. He also believes that the stock market is not always rational. Here is what Mr. Buffett says about the fictional Mr. Market in a letter to his shareholders:

Ben Graham, my friend and teacher, long ago described the mental attitude toward market fluctuations that I believe to be most conducive to investment success. He said that you should imagine market quotations as coming from a remarkably accommodating fellow named Mr. Market who is your partner in a private business.

Without fail, Mr. Market appears daily and names a price at which he will either buy your interest or sell you his.

Even though the business that the two of you own may have economic characteristics that are stable, Mr. Market's quotations will be anything but. For, sad to say, the poor fellow has incurable emotional problems. At times he feels euphoric and can see only the favorable factors affecting the business. When in that mood, he names a very high buy-sell price because he fears that you will snap up his interest and rob him of imminent gains. At other times he is depressed and can see nothing but trouble ahead for both the business and the world. On these occasions he will name a very low price, since he is terrified that you will unload your interest on him.

Mr. Market has another endearing characteristic: He doesn't mind being ignored. If his quotation is uninteresting to you today, he will be back with a new one tomorrow. Transactions are strictly at your option. Under these conditions, the more manic-depressive his behavior, the better for you.

But, like Cinderella at the ball, you must heed one warning or everything will turn into pumpkins and mice: Mr. Market is there to serve you, not to guide you. It is his pocketbook, not his wisdom that you will find useful. If he shows up some day in a particularly foolish mood, you are free to ignore him or to take advantage of him, but it will be disastrous if you fall under his influence. Indeed, if you aren't certain that you understand and can value your business far better than Mr. Market, you don't belong in the game. As they say in poker, "If you've been in the game thirty minutes and you don't know who the patsy is, you're the patsy."

...[A]n investor will succeed by coupling good business judgment with an ability to insulate his thoughts and behavior from the super-contagious emotions that swirl about the marketplace. In my own efforts to stay insulated, I have found it highly useful to keep Ben's Mr. Market concept firmly in mind.[19]

As discussed in chapter 5, the concept of weighing versus voting is based upon the concept that ultimately the value of a business over the long term will be weighed. That is, the cash flows will have a calculable value. Of course, in advance, you cannot be sure what those cash flows will be. If Mr. Market is euphoric, he may make wildly optimistic assumptions significantly overpricing the underlying security. Buffett calls that voting on the value. It has little to do with the underlying value. Of course, the same thing can happen in reverse. However, in the long term, the cash flows will be what they will be. Those cash flows will be weighed and a value will ultimately be realized even if Mr. Market is depressed or euphoric between now and then.

Warren Buffett is best known for taking his own counsel. That is one of the main reasons he lives in Omaha, Nebraska. Here is what he says in his book about living there: "You can think here. You can think better about the market; you don't hear so many stories, and you can just sit and look at the stock on the desk in front of you. You can think about a lot of things."[20]

---

19 Buffett, Warren. "Chairman's Letter - 1987 - Berkshire Hathaway Inc." Berkshire Hathaway. February 29, 1988. Accessed August 20, 2018. www. berkshirehathaway.com/letters/1987.html.

20 Pollard, Ian. *Investing in Your Life: Your Biggest Investment Opportunities Are Not Necessarily Financial.* Queensland, Australia: Wrightbooks, 2009.

Buffett is a prime example of deliberate practice and acquiring world-class capabilities. He is said to read 500 pages a day, continuously compounding his knowledge base. He spends 80 percent of his day reading. Author Thomas Corley spent five years studying the daily activities of 233 rich people and 123 poor people, which he wrote about in *Rich Habits: The Daily Success Habits of Wealthy Individuals.* He found that 67 percent of the rich people limited TV time to one hour or less per day, compared to only 23 percent of the poor people.

A major mental departure of Buffett from the rest of the financial world is how he thinks about insurance. First a little background on the insurance business: The insurance business is unusual in that it receives premiums in advance of payment of claims, sometimes many years in advance. This creates a pool of money that the insurance company holds until the claims are paid out. This is called a float. Although this money is not "owned" by the insurance company, it has use of it from the time when the payments are received until the claims are paid. This can prove to be a very attractive source of income because as this float is invested, the income is for the account of the insurance company.

The other half of the insurance industry model is underwriting. Through often-sophisticated models, actuaries estimate the future policy payment amounts and timing. This information is used to calculate the premiums. If the future payout is in the insurance company's favor, and the ultimate payout is less than the premiums received over the life of the policy, it becomes an underwriting profit. If the premiums do not cover the ultimate claim, it is an underwriting loss.

Like stock market investors, the frame of mind of insurance industry executives can vary from rational to irrational.

This mental swing often depends on external factors like Wall Street pressures, etc. This can mean there are sharp differences in strategy from one period to another. The swings can result in a particular optimistic period when the insurance executives will price their insurance products to intentionally make underwriting losses. This is justified by the logic that they will make up those losses, and then some, with gains in their investment of the float. Then, invariably, the assumptions for investment gain of the float fall short and industry profitability lags, and they adjust premium pricing in the next period and underwriting profits follow. Then some new aggressive insurance executive sees "an opportunity" to gain market share by undercutting premiums and the cycle repeats, over and over.

By thinking deeply, Buffett turned this model on its head. In retrospect, it is straightforward. Berkshire writes more policies when prices are high and fewer when prices are low. As an example, in 1984 Berkshire's largest property and casualty insurer wrote $62.2 million in policies, and premium volumes grew to $366.2 million two years later. By 1989, they had fallen back to $98.4 million and did not return to the $100 million level for twelve years. Over this period, the business averaged an underwriting profit of 6.5 percent. The typical property and casualty insurer averaged a loss of 7 percent during this period. Because claims in the insurance business are often paid years after the premiums are received, the amount of annual underwriting doesn't have a huge effect on the float from previous years' underwriting. So, the float got bigger and bigger over the years. In 2015, Berkshire's float was $87 billion. That is $87 billion in zero cost funds to invest. It doesn't take a genius to invest profitably when *any* investment return, no matter how small, is a positive.

Think about the difference: If your funds cost 6.5 percent because of underwriting losses, you therefore have to make up for that loss before your business overall is profitable. In Berkshire's case, you make a profit on underwriting *and* have zero cost funds. Wow, what a difference! Why don't more people do this? Because using Berkshire's numbers, the absolute underwriting profit in 1984 was $4 million ($62.2 x 6.5%). In 1986 it was $23.8 million, ($366.2 x 6.5%), and in 1989 it was back to $6.4 million (98.4 x 6.5%). That kind of volatility can be hard to explain to Wall Street investors and analysts, who surely do not think deeply. It requires amazing discipline. Imagine the pushback from the sales force when the amount of business fluctuates that much.

Buffett on Thinking Deeply

It is "common wisdom" that diversification is good. Buffett argues otherwise. His argument is that by concentrating choices you will do more research on the companies you choose, and with fewer companies to keep track of, you will do a better job watching over them. The top-five positions in Berkshire's portfolio have typically accounted for 60 to 80 percent of total value. This compares with 10 to 20 percent for the typical mutual fund portfolio.

Buffett on Becoming World Class

Warren Buffett is famous for being patient. Here is what he says about patience:

In investments there is no such thing as a called strike. You can stand there at the plate and the pitcher can throw a ball right down the middle, and if it's General Motors at $47

and you don't know enough to decide on GM at $47, then
you let it go right on by and no one's going to call a strike.
The only way you can have a strike is to swing and miss.[21]

His baseball analogy is right on the money. In investing, doing less is often superior to doing more.

The concept of sitting on your hands and doing nothing from an investment activity standpoint takes real discipline. Buffett said, "You do things when the opportunities come along. I've had periods in my life when I've had a bundle of ideas come along, and I've had long dry spells. If I get an idea next week, I'll do something. If not, I won't do a damn thing."

In addition to waiting years for the insurance industry pricing to become attractive, there are other important examples of his extreme patience. In the late 1990s running up to the 2000 dot.com meltdown, Buffett was severely criticized, as he was amassing billions in cash. Critics argued that Berkshire wasn't a bank and shouldn't be holding billions in cash when the tech industry was so attractive. In fact, Berkshire shares traded down from $84,000 per share in 1998 to $43,000 in 2000. Buffett was thought by many as a has-been. Of course we all know the ending to that story. In the early part of the 2000s, Buffett put that cash to work and the stock recovered and now trades over $250,000 per share. Buffett was back on top; patience paid off.

Talk about patient, long-term investment strategies. Buffett made $62.7 billion of his $63.3 billion net worth after his fiftieth birthday; 99 percent was made after his sixtieth birthday.

---

21 Lowe, Janet. *Warren Buffett Speaks: Wit and Wisdom from the World's Greatest Investor.* Hoboken, NJ: Wiley, 2007.

Buffett on Passion

Yes, passion is a major principle of The Formula. Buffett is a prime example of passion at work in creating greatness. Here's what he said on the subject:

Find your passion. I was very, very lucky to find it when I was seven or eight years old . . . You're lucky in life when you find it. And you can't guarantee you'll find it in your first job out. But I always tell college students that come out [to Omaha], "Take the job you would take if you were independently wealthy. You're going to do well at it."[22]

Buffett on Thinking Like an Owner

As you have learned, in business, thinking like an owner is really important. It can't be just an intellectual exercise. I am sure you can think of examples where you received poor service and thought, *If the owner was here it would be different.* That's exactly the attitude you should bring to any position. Own it! Here's what Buffet says about thinking like an owner:

I always picture myself as owning the whole place. And if management is following the same policy that I would follow if I owned the whole place, that's a management I like. I tell everybody who works for our company to do only two things to be successful. They are: 1) to think like an owner, and 2) tell us the bad news right away. There is no reason to worry about the good news.[23]

---

22 Safaei, Hamid. *Your Journey to Fulfillment: A Step-by-Step Guide to Realizing Your Dreams.* Amstelveen, Netherlands: ImOcean Academy, 2017.

23 Buffett, Warren. Chairman's Letter Berkshire Hathaway Annual Report.

CHAPTER 11

Steve Jobs

Talk to the very large number of people who not only worked at Apple, but worked at Apple for a very long time, and they all say the same things: "I did the best work of my life at Apple. My work had the biggest impact. I built products that are so much better than anything else I've ever done. I learned the most. And it wasn't just me; I was surrounded by the best people."

—MARC ANDERSON, FROM THE FOREWORD
OF *BECOMING STEVE JOBS*

Steve Jobs personifies The Formula. He dreamed big as few others have. He spent a lifetime pursuing his dream. His passion was legendary. And he was a very deep thinker. What sets Jobs apart from our other heroes is the number of times he failed and turned defeat into victory.

Think of Steve Jobs sitting in his garage thinking about what Apple's goal should be: Make money, get rich, make a great computer, maybe even become a "real" company? Not at all. Instead he set a goal to change people's lives through his products. Talk about audacious! That audacious goal came to life with many wonderful products that did indeed change people's lives. But, those who might think Jobs is a "gift of nature," destined to succeed, miss the point. Jobs was a prime example of a flawed product that came into its own only after many trials and, especially, many more failures.

The Early Years:
1976 to 1985, Ages 21 to 30

It all began in Jobs's parents' garage in 1976, in Los Altos, California, right in the heart of Silicon Valley. There, his partner Steve Wozniak put together a circuit board with basically off-the-shelf components. Together, they sold semifinished computers through hobbyist networks and caught the early wave of personal computing where there was little competition. Revenues were $7.8 million in 1978, $47 million in 1979, and in 1980, the year of Apple's initial public offering (IPO), revenues reached $1 billion. No other company had ever grown that fast. Their flagship product, the Apple II computer, was a raging success.

In chapter 1, we discussed the concept of the reality distortion field. It was during this early period that the term reality distortion field was coined by fellow Apple employee Bud Tribble to describe Jobs. What Tribble meant was Jobs just wouldn't take no for an answer. He seemed to "will" things to happen his way. Often fellow managers at Apple felt that what Jobs wanted to accomplish was impossible, but he convinced them it was possible.

Here is a story Walter Isaacson reported about the reality distortion field in Jobs's mature years:

At one point Steve wants to do the iPhone, but he doesn't want the face to be plastic. He wanted it to be this beautiful silky glass. Steve being Steve, he just picks up the phone and calls the Corning Glass switchboard and says,

"Let me speak to your CEO." The switchboard says, "Fine, we'll take your name and number." He says, "Typical East Coast bullshit," and slams down the phone. Wendell Weeks, the Corning CEO, is a cool guy. He hears about it, and he picks up the phone, calls the switchboard at [Apple Headquarters in] Cupertino, and says, "Let me speak to your CEO." They say, "Will you fax your request in writing?" It gets back to Steve, and Steve says, "I like this guy."

They have a meeting, and Steve says, "I want this type of glass." Weeks says, "Well, we once did a process called Gorilla Glass that has this ion transfer. It'd be kind of good, but we never made it."

And Steve looked at the process, said, "Yeah, that's what I want. I want this much by September, and do it secretly."

And Wendell says, "Well, I just told you, we've never made it before. We don't have the capacity." And Steve just stares at him, unblinking, and says, "Don't be afraid. You can do it." And they did. He [Steve] had what they called a "reality distortion field," and it compelled people to do amazing things that they thought were impossible.[24]

Remember the concept of heuristics discussed in chapter 6? Due to the inability of our subconscious to process inputs real time, humans take shortcuts. The narrative heuristic is one of the most powerful. In this heuristic perspective, our subconscious hears well-told, believable stories as fact, even when they are not true. In this case, Jobs was so proficient in spinning his logic in the form of a narrative, or story, that even when wrong, he could convince those around him to believe. The result is that his colleagues often accomplished far more than any of them imagined.

---

24 Isaacson, Walter. *Steve Jobs*. New York, NY: Simon & Schuster, 2011.

Jobs was a great persuader from a very young age. When he was in eighth grade, he decided to build a frequency counter for a school project and needed parts. Someone suggested he call Bill Hewlett, co-founder of the Hewlett-Packard Company. After finding a William Hewlett in the telephone book, Jobs called and asked, "Is this the Bill Hewlett of Hewlett-Packard?" Several days later, Jobs went to HP and picked up a bag full of parts that Hewlett had put together for him. He was then offered an internship for that summer. He was twelve years old.

Nolan Bushnell, founder of Atari, who hired Jobs in 1974, says what he remembers most about Jobs was his intensity. He says:

> *Steve was the first guy I found who would be regularly curled up under his desk in the morning after an all-nighter. A lot of people think that success is luck and being in the right place at the right time. But I think if you're willing to work harder than anybody else, you can create an awful lot of your own luck.*[25]

In this context, Jobs was really gifted in his drive and vision, but he was almost equally flawed, as he couldn't see Apple's accomplishments in the context of his team. He had to be the smartest man in the room, which resulted in repeated product failures, following Apple II's blockbuster success. Jobs pushed so hard and was so ruthless that his board continuously cautioned him to be more inclusive and collaborative, until ultimately he was fired from Apple. Jobs

---

25 Guglielmo, Connie. "Untold Stories About Steve Jobs: Friends and Colleagues Share Their Memories." *Forbes.* October 3, 2012. Accessed August 20, 2018. www.forbes.com/sites/connieguglielmo/2012/10/03/untold-stories-about-steve-jobs-friends-and-colleagues-share-their-memories/#d13daf46c584.

was the ultimate case of the brilliant deviant being expelled by the traditionalists.

History has shown that he was not ready to become the Steve Jobs that changed the world through his products. His skills just were not scalable. He couldn't possibly have better judgment than his coworkers in engineering, software, and all the other myriad of areas under him, especially as he wasn't trained in any of these sciences. He had fallen into the trap of being "a genius and a thousand helpers." But he hadn't learned that yet, so he had to fail. This is what makes Steve Jobs even more interesting as a subject of The Formula. Learning on the job is a central feature of The Formula. The whole idea is to use the time inherent in a marathon and to enhance our capabilities with our passion and deep thinking, learning to gain insights others simply can't see.

The Wilderness Years:
1986 to 1996, Ages 31 to 41

When Jobs left Apple in 1985, he sold every Apple share he owned for $70 million, save one, so he could attend shareholder meetings. A year later he invested $10 million in a tiny group of computer graphics experts that were getting spun out of Lucasfilm of *Star Wars* fame, owned by George Lucas. The new company was led by Ed Catmull and John Lasseter, who had been running that division at Lucasfilm. The problem was, there wasn't really a company or a product. While at Lucasfilm, Catmull and Lasseter developed a computer prototype that was very advanced at computer animation. Jobs's investment thesis was to begin selling their creation—the Pixar Image Computer—that sold for over a hundred thousand dollars each. Their computer showed promise in computer graphics, which could create lifelike images. This is another example of an investment that went very wrong but, through the principles of The Formula, eventually became very right, thereby avoiding another failure.

The problem with Jobs's plan was that Catmull and Lasseter were not computer folks; they were animators at heart. Jobs was a computer guy, and his experience was with personal computers, which was a very different animal from the very sophisticated hundred-thousand-dollar computer being planned. What Catmull and Lasseter really wanted to do was build an animation studio along the lines of Walt Disney Animation Studio. The notion was a far cry from a computer manufacturer. But try they did. They built a factory, hired a sales force, and spent five years trying to sell their computers. Ultimately, they sold only 300 computers. By 1991 Jobs had funded their losses by investing more than $50 million, a significant portion of his net worth.

During the period from 1986 to 1991, the Pixar team experimented with making short films and commercials using computer animation. They had artistic success. In 1988 their short film *Tin Toy* won an Academy Award. In 1991 the team gave up on the mission of selling computers and laid off the people involved. Instead Jobs, Catmull, and Lasseter committed everything to building an animation studio. This was an amazing leap of faith, but this is where all the passion from Catmull and Lasseter resided. They would struggle mightily, but were able to convince Disney CEO Michael Eisner of their special talent. This resulted in Disney underwriting the cost of producing their first feature-length animated film, *Toy Story*. In 1995 *Toy Story* opened to critical and box office success, and Pixar went public at a valuation of $1.5 billion. Jobs's original investment was worth over $1 billion. Pixar's future was assured. Ultimately, the Pixar-Disney relationship would prove hugely beneficial to both sides.

In the beginning, Jobs and Disney CEO Michael Eisner had huge battles over control of the movies and split of the profits, and it looked at certain points that the two companies would split their profitable partnership. But, ultimately, Jobs and Bob Iger, Disney's next CEO, formed a close friendship, leading to Disney's acquisition of Pixar for $7.4 billion and Jobs's appointment to Disney's board as its largest shareholder. This was a new Steve Jobs.

In Ed Catmull's book, *Creativity, Inc.: Overcoming the Unseen Forces That Stand in the Way of True Inspiration*, John Lasseter is quoted as saying: "Steve's story is the classic Hero's Journey. Banished for his hubris from the company he founded, he wandered through the wilderness having a series of adventures that, in the end, changed him for the better. Failure made him better, wiser, and kinder."[26]

Just as Pixar morphed into something completely different from the original investment thesis, gaining victory from the jaws of defeat, so did Jobs's second investment during this period. Jobs founded NeXT shortly after leaving Apple. NeXT was a workstation computer, much more powerful than the Macs. NeXT was designed to be used by scientists and engineers to perform heavy-duty calculations or mathematical models. Steve and his management team worked mightily trying to design and sell workstations, but the competitive dynamics were much more difficult than in the early days of Apple.

Ultimately, after eight years of slugging it out in the workstation market, NeXT threw in the towel and closed its hardware division, laying off half its employees. By this time investors had $350 million invested in the company,

---

26 Catmull, Ed, and Amy Wallace. Creativity, Inc.: *Overcoming The Unseen Forces That Stand in the Way of True Inspiration*. New York, NY: Random House, 2014.

and Jobs feared the entire amount might be lost. However, in another escape from defeat, even as much as the hardware of NeXT was unsuccessful, the company had developed two very good software products and would focus on the software business going forward: NeXTSTEP was an operating system that the company licensed to other computer makers; and WebObjects was a tool for building websites. Revenues from these products enabled the company to make a small operating profit, and it started exploring an initial public offering (IPO).

When Steve was fired from Apple in 1985 and replaced by "professional management," it had been only nine years after he co-founded Apple. That same year Apple earned $60 million. Over the next eleven years, three separate "professional CEOs" tried to lead Apple. Ultimately, they were all unsuccessful. By 1996, Apple suffered a $1 billion loss and was considering bankruptcy. Their problems were further complicated by a failed effort over the previous eight years to update its operating system software architecture. Apple's dilemma, the strength of the NeXTSTEP operating system, and the outstanding team of designers at NeXT drove a $429 million buyout of NeXT by Apple in December 1996. Jobs rejoined Apple as an advisor. Eight months after the transaction, the existing Apple CEO was out and Jobs was the CEO.

The Mature Jobs:
1997 to 2011, Ages 42 to 56

Apple's board of directors had to be desperate. There was nothing in Jobs's background that would suggest he had the skillset to turn Apple around. Nothing, that is, but vision and passion. Jobs loved Apple. He believed in its prospects. And, as important, he was a changed man. Gone was the erratic, impetuous "genius and a thousand helpers." During the wilderness years of his Hero's Journey, Jobs had matured into a far more contemplative, team-oriented leader. He had always had the knack for enticing super-talented people to join the cause. But now he would enable them to use their full talents, which as a collective, no person could match, not even Steve Jobs. As a result they stayed together as a team and created arguably the most effective product innovation powerhouse ever.

Over the next fourteen years, until he passed away in 2011 of pancreatic cancer at age fifty-six, Jobs led perhaps the greatest success story in business history, taking a company that had lost a billion dollars the year he rejoined to making Apple the most valuable company in any industry in the world, worth over $500 billion!

Steve Jobs illustrates very well what I refer to as the Mr. Potato Head philosophy. Mr. Potato Head is a children's toy invented in the 1950s. Each of the body parts—ears, nose, legs, etc.—have little plastic pegs in them that could be used to place them on a potato to make a person's face with the potato as the body. Accessories like hats and glasses could be bought as supplements to create a very inexpensive toy. You could choose from the many options of body parts to create a custom toy. You did not have to like all the body parts or accessories; you could choose the ones you liked and disregard the rest.

Here's how Mr. Potato Head applies to Steve Jobs. Jobs was a very controversial character. His passion and drive could sometimes feel abusive, especially to folks who were traditionalists or people who lacked commitment to the cause. This led some people to misunderstand him and totally disregard him. My point is, don't lose sight of his behavior. Take the parts of Jobs you can learn from and admire, and disregard the rest. I always look for the one or two character-istics of an individual I admire and emulate them.

Vic Gundotra, Google's former senior vice president, relayed a story in a social-media post about Jobs. One Sunday morning he received a call from Jobs questioning the color of the second "O" in Google on the iPhone, which was about to be released. Here is what he said about that experience upon Jobs's passing: "When I think about leadership, passion, and attention to detail, I think back to the call I received from Steve Jobs on a Sunday morning in January. It was a lesson I'll never forget. CEOs should care about details. Even shades of yellow. On a Sunday."[27]

27 Gundotra, Vic. "Icon Ambulance." Google+. August 25, 2011. Accessed August 20, 2018. plus.google.com/+VicGundotra/posts/gcSStkKxXTw.

Conclusion

In the years prior to 2007, as a public company, MacDermid was faced with many onerous requirements, mostly under the Sarbanes–Oxley legislation enacted in 2002. This federal law made public companies more accountable for their actions. However, all the legislation really did was create red tape and bureaucracy. For a company MacDermid's size, the new requirements consumed far too much of the CEO's time. Ultimately, in the biggest mistake of my life, we went private.

The theory was we would go under the radar for a few years and come back as a new public company with the scale such that the requirements of the regulations under Sarbanes–Oxley wouldn't be so onerous. I had a commitment from the partners of the private equity fund to underwrite this strategy. The result would have been a public offering of our shares (IPO).

In 2013 I spent six months visiting investors in preparation for the IPO. The idea was to clearly communicate our values and strategy and see if there were larger shareholders who were aligned with us and who would commit to large blocks of stock. I really worked this hard, while crisscrossing the United States and Canada.

One of my favorite vignettes from this effort was my attempt to meet with a very large insurance company's chief investment officer. The problem was he didn't invest in

IPOs. But I just knew our companies were well aligned and he would love our story, so I came up with a way to arrange a meeting with him. I asked his assistant to pass on the following message: "I want an hour, and if the hour is not one of the most compelling ever, I will write a personal check for five thousand dollars to the insurance company's favorite charity."

I got the meeting; he loved the story of how we planned to take MacDermid to the next level and wanted in. *Yee-haw!*

Toward the end of the process of lining up investors for the impending IPO, we presented the IPO details to our private equity partners. To my absolute shock, the lead partner said he didn't want to do an IPO. And since they held control, that was the end of the IPO. At that moment, I realized the 2007 go-private transaction was a mistake and I had lost control of the clan I was entrusted to preserve.

Later, we were approached by Platform, a special purpose acquisition company (SPAC), which is basically a pool of public money formed to buy a specific company. At first it seemed like it was our answer to going public. But, as we were progressing toward a closing of a transaction with them, I began to see a pattern I was uncomfortable with. It was becoming more and more obvious to me and others on the management team at MacDermid that there would be a clash of cultures with the folks behind Platform.

I tried to get out of the transaction, but under threats by the lead private equity partner, I relented, and we closed the transaction. I tried to work with these new owners, but the culture clash was just too great, and within two years, I felt I had to resign, which was called retirement. I am the first to admit that MacDermid's culture is unique. Much of this book is about that. I also accept that our culture was not a fit with the new owners. It doesn't make them wrong, just different.

The fault wasn't with the new owners; it was with the private equity firm that broke its promises.

Platform was paying me a huge salary. Yes, I could have just gone through the motions and collected my pay. However, as you have likely sensed throughout this book, I couldn't do that. My principles wouldn't allow it. I left with my honor intact, and job offers came streaming in. Ultimately, I became Operating Partner in a private equity fund where I use the principles of The Formula to help companies and management teams achieve their dreams.

As I approach my seventieth year, I reflect back on my journey. Starting as a learning-disabled little boy, I have made the most of the hand I was dealt. As my mom said after Mac-Dermid became a major success, "Who would have thunk?" Through many trials and tribulations, I have survived the ridicule that comes from my weaknesses and enjoyed the triumphs of success. This has been a well-satisfying journey made possible by the principles of The Formula. I can't help but believe that if I could use these principles to my level of success, it is possible for anyone, including you.

Honestly as flawed a person as I am, I wouldn't expect you to believe that following my lead is the answer. That is why I have tried to include the science and other examples of successful people who used the principles of The Formula to great success. I wish you a joyful journey.

Recommended Reading

Best All-Time Recommendations

Rand, Ayn. *Atlas Shrugged.* Penguin, 2005.

Rand, Ayn. *The Fountainhead.* Penguin, 2005.

Books about Thinking

Chabris, Christopher, and Daniel Simons. *The Invisible Gorilla: How Our Intuitions Deceive Us.* Harmony, 2011.

Duke, Annie. *Thinking in Bets: Making Smarter Decisions When You Don't Have All the Facts.* Penguin, 2018.

Hayek, F.A. *The Road to Serfdom.* University of Chicago Press, 2007.

Kahneman, Daniel. *Thinking, Fast and Slow.* Farrar, Straus, and Giroux, 2013.

Taleb, Nassim Nicholas. *Antifragile: Things That Gain from Disorder.* Random House, 2014.

Taleb, Nassim Nicholas. *Fooled by Randomness: The Hidden Role of Chance in Life and in the Markets.* Random House, 2005.

Taleb, Nassim Nicholas. *Skin in the Game: Hidden Asymmetries in Daily Life.* Random House, 2018.

Taleb, Nassim Nicholas. *The Black Swan: The Impact of the Highly Improbable.* Random House, 2010.

Books about Human Physiology and Performance

Ashton, Kevin. *How to Fly a Horse: The Secret History of Creation, Invention, and Discovery.* Anchor Books, 2015.

Begley, Sharon. *Train Your Mind, Change Your Brain: How a New Science Reveals Our Extraordinary Potential to Transform Ourselves.* Ballantine Books, 2007.

Blackburn, PhD, Elizabeth, and Elissa Epel, PhD. *The Telomere Effect: A Revolutionary Approach to Living Younger, Healthier, Longer.* Grand Central Publishing, 2018.

Breuning, PhD, Loretta Graziano. *Habits of a Happy Brain: Retrain Your Brain to Boost Your Serotonin, Dopamine, Oxytocin, & Endorphin Levels.* Adams Media, 2015.

Cain, Susan. *Quiet: The Power of Introverts in a World That Can't Stop Talking.* Random House, 2013.

Colvin, Geoffrey. *Talent Is Overrated: What Really Separates World-Class Performers from Everybody Else.* Portfolio, 2010.

Coyle, Daniel. *Culture Code: The Secrets of Highly Successful Groups.* Bantam Books, 2018.

Coyle, Daniel. *The Talent Code: Greatness Isn't Born. It's Grown. Here's How.* New York, NY: Bantam Books, 2009.

Csikszentmihalyi, Mihaly. *Flow: The Psychology of Optimal Experience.* Harper Perennial Modern Classics, 2008.

Cuddy, Amy. *Presence: Bringing Your Boldest Self to Your Biggest Challenges.* Little, Brown and Company, 2015.

Duckworth, Angela. *Grit: The Power of Passion and Perseverance.* Scribner, 2016.

Duhigg, Charles. *The Power of Habit: Why We Do What We Do in Life and Business.* Random House, 2014.

Dweck, Carol S. *Mindset: The New Psychology of Success.* Random House, 2007.

Epstein, David. *The Sports Gene: Inside the Science of Extraordinary Athletic Performance.* Penguin Group, 2014.

Ericsson, Anders, and Robert Pool. *Peak: Secrets from the New Science of Expertise.* Houghton Mifflin Harcourt, 2017.

Frankl, Viktor E. *Man's Search for Meaning.* Beacon Press, 2014.

Gazzaniga, Michael S. *Tales from Both Sides of the Brain: A Life in Neuroscience.* HarperCollins, 2015.

Gladwell, Malcom. *Blink: The Power of Thinking Without Thinking.* Little, Brown and Company, 2007.

Gladwell, Malcom. *David and Goliath: Underdogs, Misfits, and the Art of Battling Giants.* Little, Brown and Company, 2013.

Gladwell, Malcom. *Outliers: The Story of Success.* Little, Brown and Company, 2008.

Gladwell, Malcom. *The Tipping Point: How Little Things Can Make a Big Difference.* Little, Brown and Company, 2006.

Grant, Adam. *Originals: How Nonconformists Move the World.* Penguin Books, 2017.

Hari, Johann. *Lost Connections: Uncovering the Real Causes of Depression—and the Unexpected Solutions.* Bloomsbury, 2018.

Hawkins, Jeff, and Sara Blakeslee. *On Intelligence: How a New Understanding of the Brain Will Lead to the Creation of Truly Intelligent Machines.* St. Martin's Griffin, 2005.

Kaku, Michio. *The Future of the Mind: The Scientific Quest to Understand, Enhance, and Empower the Mind.* Anchor Books, 2015.

Kotler, Steven, and Jamie Wheal. *Stealing Fire: How Silicon Valley, the Navy SEALS, and Maverick Scientists Are Revolutionizing the Way We Live and Work.* Dey Street Books, 2018.

Kotler, Steven. *The Rise of Superman: Decoding the Science of Ultimate Human Performance.* Houghton Mifflin Harcourt, 2014.

Pink, Daniel H. *A Whole New Mind: Why Right-Brainers Will Rule the Future.* Riverhead Books, 2006.

Pink, Daniel H. *Drive: The Surprising Truth About What Motivates Us.* Riverhead Books, 2009.

Ramo, Joshua Cooper. *The Age of the Unthinkable: Why the New World Disorder Constantly Surprises Us and What We Can Do About It.* Little, Brown and Company, 2009.

Ratey, MD, John J., with Eric Hagerman. *Spark: The Revolutionary New Science of Exercise and the Brain.* Little, Brown and Company, 2008.

Roth, Bernard. *The Achievement Habit: Stop Wishing, Start Doing, and Take Command of Your Life.* HarperCollins, 2015.

Sapolsky, Robert M. *Behave: The Biology of Humans at Our Best and Worst.* Penguin, 2018.

Shaywitz, MD, Sally. *Overcoming Dyslexia: A New and Complete Science-Based Program for Reading Problems at Any Level.* Random House, 2005.

Sneed, Brandon. *Head in the Game: The Mental Engineering of the World's Greatest Athletes.* HarperCollins, 2017.

Stulberg, Brad, and Steve Magness. *Peak Performance: Elevate Your Game, Avoid Burnout, and Thrive with the New Science of Success.* Rodale Books, 2017.

Syed, Matthew. *Black Box Thinking: Why Most People Never Learn from Their Mistakes—But Some Do.* Penguin, 2015.

Syed, Matthew. *Bounce: Mozart, Federer, Picasso, Beckham, and the Science of Success.* Harper Collins, 2011.

Thaler, Richard H., and Cass R. Sunstein. *Nudge: Improving Decisions about Health, Wealth, and Happiness.* Yale University Press, 2008.

Tracy, Brian. *Insights into Achievement.* Nightingale-Conant, 1996.

Tracy, Brian. *Maximum Achievement: Strategies and Skills That Will Unlock Your Hidden Powers to Succeed.* New York, NY: Simon & Schuster, 1995.

Wolf, Maryanne. *Proust and the Squid: The Story and Science of the Reading Brain.* Harper Perennial, 2008.

Biographies of Unusual People

Chernow, Ron. *The House of Morgan: An American Banking Dynasty and the Rise of Modern Finance.* Grove Press, 2010.

Chernow, Ron. *The Warburgs: The Twentieth-Century Odyssey of a Remarkable Jewish Family.* Random House, 2016.

Chernow, Ron. *Titan: The Life of John D. Rockefeller, Sr.* Vintage, 2004.

Isaacson, Walter. *Benjamin Franklin: An American Life.* Simon & Schuster, 2004.

Isaacson, Walter. *Einstein: His Life and Universe.* Simon & Schuster, 2017.

Isaacson, Walter. *Leonardo Da Vinci.* Simon & Schuster, 2017.

Isaacson, Walter. *Steve Jobs.* Simon & Schuster, 2015.

Lowenstein, Roger. *Buffett: The Making of an American Capitalist.* Random House, 2008.

Manchester, William, and Paul Reid. *The Last Lion: Winston Spencer Churchill.* Volumes 1, 2, and 3. Little, Brown and Company, 2012.

Schlender, Brent, and Rick Tetzeli. *Becoming Steve Jobs: The Evolution of a Reckless Upstart into a Visionary Leader.* Crown Business, 2016.

Schroeder, Alice. *The Snowball: Warren Buffett and the Business of Life.* Bantam Books, 2009.

Walton, Sam, and John Huey. *Sam Walton: Made in America.* Doubleday, 1992.

Books about Business

Bock, Laszlo. *Work Rules! Insights from Inside Google That Will Transform How You Live and Lead.* Twelve, 2015.

Catmull, Ed, and Amy Wallace. *Creativity, Inc.: Overcoming the Unseen Forces That Stand in the Way of True Inspiration.* New York, NY: Random House, 2014.

Christensen, Clayton M. *The Innovator's Dilemma: When New Technologies Cause Great Firms to Fail.* Harvard Business Review Press, 2016.

Doerr, John. *Measure What Matters: How Google, Bono, and the Gates Foundation Rock the World with OKRs.* Penguin Random House, 2018.

Horowitz, Ben. *The Hard Thing about Hard Things: Building a Business When There Are No Easy Answers.* HarperBusiness, 2014.

Iddings, Sean, and Ian Cassel. *Intelligent Fanatics Project: How Great Leaders Build Sustainable Businesses.* MicroCapClub Publication, 2016.

Iddings, Sean, and Ian Cassel. *Intelligent Fanatics: Standing on the Shoulders of Giants.* Intelligent Fanatics Publication, 2017.

Levy, Steven. *In the Plex: How Google Thinks, Works, and Shapes Our Lives.* Simon & Schuster, 2011.

Lewis, Michael. *The Big Short: Inside the Doomsday Machine.* W.W. Norton & Company, 2011.

Lowenstein, Roger. *When Genius Failed: The Rise and Fall of Long-Term Capital Management.* New York, NY: Penguin Random House, 2001.

Ries, Eric. *The Startup Way: How Modern Companies Use Entrepreneurial Management to Transform Culture & Drive Long-Term Growth.* Currency, 2017.

Schmidt, Eric, and Jonathan Rosenberg. *How Google Works.* Grand Central Publishing, 2017.

Senor, Dan, and Saul Singer. *Start-up Nation: The Story of Israel's Economic Miracle.* Twelve, 2011.

Shaw, Robert Bruce. *Extreme Teams: Why Pixar, Netflix, Airbnb, and Other Cutting-Edge Companies Succeed Where Most Fail.* AMACOM, 2017.

Stone, Brad. *The Everything Store: Jeff Bezos and the Age of Amazon.* Little, Brown and Company, 2013.

Thorndike, Jr., William N. *The Outsiders: Eight Unconventional CEOs and Their Radically Rational Blueprint for Success.* Harvard Business Review Press, 2012.

Voss, Chris, and Tahl Raz. *Never Split the Difference: Negotiating as if Your Life Depended on It.* HarperBusiness, 2016.

Wodtke, Christina. *Radical Focus: Achieving Your Most Important Goals with Objectives and Key Results.* Cucina Media LLC, 2016.

References

Chapter 1

Quotes from Bill Gargano were from 2015 interview with Alan Farnham.

Chapter 2

Buffett, Mary, and David Clark. *The New Buffettology: The Proven Techniques for Investing Successfully in Changing Markets That Have Made Warren Buffett the World's Most Famous Investor.* New York, NY: Scribner, 2002.

Buffett, Mary, and David Clark. *The Tao of Warren Buffett: Warren Buffett's Words of Wisdom: Quotations and Interpretations to Help Guide You to Billionaire Wealth and Enlightened Business Management.* New York, NY: Scribner, 2006.

Buffett, Warren, and Lawrence A. Cunningham. *The Essays of Warren Buffett: Lessons for Corporate America.* Durham, NC: The Cunningham Group & Carolina Academic Press, 2015.

Hagstrom, Robert G. *The Warren Buffett Portfolio: Mastering the Power of the Focus Investment Strategy.* Hoboken, NJ: Wiley and Sons, 1999.

Lowe, Janet. *Warren Buffett Speaks: Wit and Wisdom from the World's Greatest Investor.* Hoboken, NJ: Wiley, 2007.

Schroeder, Alice. *The Snowball: Warren Buffett and the Business of Life.* New York, NY: Bantam Books, 2009.

Tracy, Brian. *Insights into Achievement.* Nightingale-Conant, 1996.

Tracy, Brian. *Maximum Achievement: Strategies and Skills That Will Unlock Your Hidden Powers to Succeed.* New York, NY: Simon & Schuster, 1995.

Tracy, Brian. *The Psychology of Achievement.* New York, NY: Simon & Schuster, 2002. Audiobook.

Walton, Sam, and John Huey. *Sam Walton: Made in America.* New York, NY: Doubleday, 1992.

Chapter 3

Csikszentmihalyi, Mihaly. *Flow: The Psychology of Optimal Experience.* New York, NY: Harper Perennial Modern Classics, 2008.

Tracy, Brian. *Maximum Achievement: Strategies and Skills That Will Unlock Your Hidden Powers to Succeed.* New York, NY: Simon & Schuster, 1995.

Chapter 4

Ballard, Ian C., Vishnu P. Murty, R. McKell Carter, Jeffrey J. MacInnes, Scott A. Huettel, and R. Alison Adcock. "Dorsolateral Prefrontal Cortex Drives Mesolimbic Dopaminergic Regions to Initiate Motivated Behavior." *Journal of Neuroscience* 31, no. 28 (July 2011): 10340–46. doi.org/10.1523/JNEUROSCI.0895-11.2011.

Csikszentmihalyi, Mihaly. *Flow: The Psychology of Optimal Experience.* New York, NY: Harper Perennial Modern Classics, 2008.

Kotler, Steven, and Jamie Wheal. *Stealing Fire: How Silicon Valley, the Navy SEALS, and Maverick Scientists Are Revolutionizing the Way We Live and Work.* New York, NY: Dey Street Books, 2018.

Kotler, Steven. *The Rise of Superman: Decoding the Science of Ultimate Human Performance.* Boston, MA: Houghton Mifflin Harcourt, 2014.

Chapter 5

Coyle, Daniel. *The Talent Code: Greatness Isn't Born. It's Grown. Here's How.* New York, NY: Bantam Books, 2009.

Ericsson, Anders, and Robert Pool. *Peak: Secrets from the New Science of Expertise.* Boston, MA: Houghton Mifflin Harcourt, 2017.

Chapter 6

Center for Open Science. "Massive Collaboration Testing Reproducibility of Psychology Studies Publishes Findings." COS.io. August 27, 2015. Accessed August 20, 2018. cos.io/about/news/massive-collaboration-testing-reproducibility-psychology-studies-publishes-findings/.

Kahneman, Daniel. *Thinking, Fast and Slow*. New York, NY: Farrar, Straus, and Giroux, 2013.

Lowenstein, Roger. *When Genius Failed: The Rise and Fall of Long-Term Capital Management*. New York, NY: Penguin Random House, 2001.

Taleb, Nassim Nicholas. *The Black Swan: The Impact of the Highly Improbable*. New York, NY: Random House, 2010.

Chapter 7

Collins, Jim, and Jerry I. Porras, Jerry. *Built to Last: Successful Habits of Visionary Companies*. New York, NY: HarperBusiness, 2004.

Chapter 9

Walton, Sam, and John Huey. *Sam Walton: Made in America*. New York, NY: Doubleday, 1992.

Chapter 10

Buffett, Mary, and David Clark. *The New Buffettology: The Proven Techniques for Investing Successfully in Changing Markets That Have Made Warren Buffett the World's Most Famous Investor*. New York, NY: Scribner, 2002.

Buffett, Mary, and David Clark. *The Tao of Warren Buffett: Warren Buffett's Words of Wisdom: Quotations and Interpretations to Help Guide You to Billionaire Wealth and Enlightened Business Management*. New York, NY: Scribner, 2006.

Buffett, Warren, and Lawrence A. Cunningham. *The Essays of Warren Buffett: Lessons For Corporate America*. Durham, NC: The Cunningham Group & Carolina Academic Press, 2015.

Corley, Thomas, C. *Rich Habits: The Daily Success Habits of Wealthy Individuals.* Minneapolis, MN: Langdon Street Press, 2010.

Graham, Benjamin, Jason Zwieg, and Warren Buffett. *The Intelligent Investor: The Definitive Book on Value Investing.* New York, NY: HarperBusiness, 2006.

Hagstrom, Robert G. *The Warren Buffett Portfolio: Mastering the Power of the Focus Investment Strategy.* Hoboken, NJ: Wiley and Sons, 1999.

Lowenstein, Roger. *Buffett: The Making of an American Capitalist.* New York, NY: Random House, 2008.

Schroeder, Alice. *The Snowball: Warren Buffett and the Business of Life.* New York, NY: Bantam Books, 2009.

Chapter 11

Catmull, Ed, and Amy Wallace. *Creativity, Inc.: Overcoming the Unseen Forces That Stand in the Way of True Inspiration.* New York, NY: Random House, 2014.

Isaacson, Walter. *Steve Jobs.* New York, NY: Simon & Schuster, 2011.

Schlender, Brent, Rick Tetzeli, and Marc Andreessen. *Becoming Steve Jobs: The Evolution of a Reckless Upstart into a Visionary Leader.* New York, NY: Crown Business, 2016.

Acknowledgments

There are so many to thank.

First and foremost I owe gratitude to my mom and dad, who nurtured me through many very tough years. Clearly I would not have become who I am without their love and devotion.

There are so many colleagues at MacDermid over my thirty-five years who carried me on their shoulders; it is impossible to list them all. To all of the Clan MacDermid, my eternal thanks.

Tom Smith taught me nearly everything I know about business. Thank you, Tom. I will be forever grateful.

To my friend and loyal supporter Quinn Spitzer, thank you for your friendship and encouragement.

To my brother Andy who started our professional journey together, keep smiling, I love you.

A special thank-you goes out to Sharon Johnson, my longtime assistant and partner in my journey.

To my partner, Dave Ferguson, who inspired me to write this book, thanks for the encouragement.

Thank you to Art LoVetere for giving me my start at MacDermid. I admire your life's mission. You are a good man.

To my collaborators, Alan Farnham, who helped me with early content, and Michele Matrisciani the development editor who worked tirelessly to make sense of my rambling, and to The Book Couple, Carol Killman Rosenberg, my copyeditor, and her husband, Gary, who created the cover and interior design, thank you for humoring me as a first-time author. This book is a far better product because of your inputs. Thank you.

About the Author

Dan Leever is a Operating Partner at PWP Growth Equity, a private equity firm affiliated with Perella Weinberg Partners, where he focuses on investments in industrial businesses. Prior to PWP Growth Equity, he spent more than thirty years growing specialty chemical companies. He served as CEO of Platform Specialty Products Corporation (PSP) of West Palm Beach, Florida, and was associated with its predecessor companies since 1983.

PSP is a multinational specialty chemical manufacturer with revenues of $3.7 billion, over 8,500 employees, and operations in 100 countries. In 1990, Leever was appointed president and chief executive officer and, in 1998, chairman and chief executive officer of MacDermid Inc., the predecessor to PSP. During his tenure as CEO, MacDermid increased revenues fivefold while shareholder value increased by twenty times. In 2007, Leever led the buyout of MacDermid as a public entity and, in 2013, participated in the acquisition of MacDermid by PSP, which was listed on the New York Stock Exchange in 2014.

Leever attended Kansas State University from 1968 to 1971 where he studied business. He received an MBA from the University of New Haven Graduate School of Business in 1999.

Leever is founder and chairman of Vail Snow Sports Foundation and TA Foundation—nonprofit organizations dedicated to promoting youth snow sports through financial support to young athletes. He formerly served on the board of the U.S. Ski and Snowboard Association, the governing body of U.S. Olympic skiing and snowboarding, and currently serves on the board of Ski and Snowboard Club Vail.

Leever is married with two grown sons and two grandchildren.